PRAISE FOR KAFKA'S AX

In this tour de force, Kaminsky wields his own ax against the iconic "Kafka," the classic modernist we think we know. Smashing that idol in the book's multiple collaged texts, poetry and prose, Kaminsky restores the shattered, impossibly cohering fragments of Kafka's own being.

—PHILIP FRIED, author of *Interrogating Water and other poems* and editor of *The Manhattan Review*

For Kafka, writing was an ax to break the frozen sea within. And so it is with Kaminsky's work, dipping and diving into twists and turns of Kafka's being, particularly his inner life – our inner life. Through poetry, prose, reflection, speculation and documentation, we are led to awe and appreciation for psycho-spiritual reality. We meet faces that seek us and a wind-swept visage challenges us to evolve further, if we can, if we dare, and we must. *Kafka's Ax* eggs us on to the far side of our lives, nothing closer or more intimate, whirls of opacity and transparency that tear us with wonder.

—MICHAEL EIGEN, author of *Under the Totem: In Search of a Path* and *Contact with the Depths*

In *Kafka's Ax*, Marc Kaminsky interweaves prose fiction and poetry with such grace and such remarkable feats of imaginative and sometimes parodic mimicry that one is never entirely sure of the border between genres. This book is for anyone who appreciates the craft of writing and how the language of poetry and prose can come together.

—JACK KUGELMASS, author of *The Miracle of Intervale Avenue*

OTHER BOOKS BY MARC KAMINISKY

POETRY

The Stones of Lifta (2019)
A Cleft in the Rock (2018)
Shadow Traffic (2018)
Target Populations (1991)
The Road from Hiroshima (1984)
Daily Bread (1982)
A Table with People (1982)
A New House (1974)

PROSE

What's Inside You It Shines Out of You (1974)

EDITOR

Stories as Equipment for Living: Last Talks and Tales by Barbara Myerhoff. Co-edited with Mark Weiss in collaboration with Deena Metzger (2007)
Remembered Lives: The Work of Ritual, Storytelling and Growing Older, by Barbara Myerhoff (1992)
The Uses of Reminiscence (1984)
The Book of Autobiographies (1982)
The Journal Project: Pages from the Lives of Old People (1980)

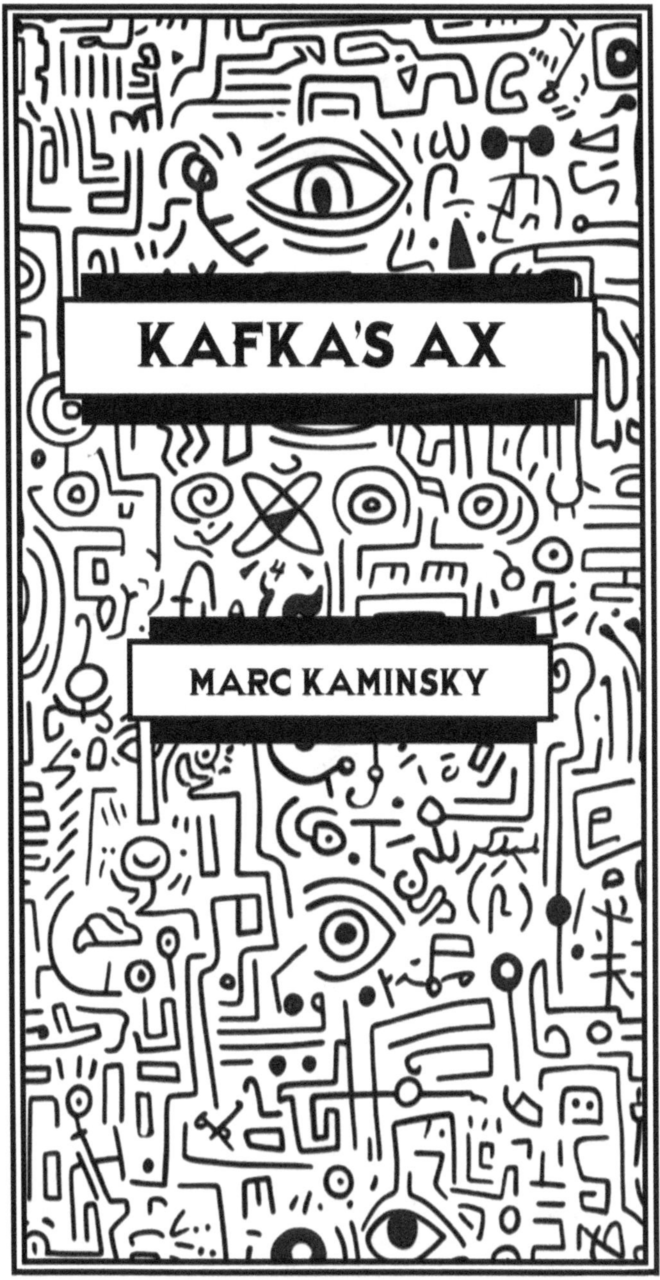

KAFKA'S AX

MARC KAMINSKY

DOS MADRES

2025

DOS MADRES PRESS INC.

P.O. Box 294, Loveland, Ohio 45140
www.dosmadres.com   editor@dosmadres.com

Dos Madres is dedicated to the belief that the small press is essential to the vitality of contemporary literature as a carrier of the new voice, as well as the older, sometimes forgotten voices of the past. And in an ever more virtual world, to the creation of fine books pleasing to the eye and hand.

Dos Madres is named in honor of Vera Murphy and Libbie Hughes, the "Dos Madres" whose contributions have made this press possible.

Dos Madres Press, Inc. is an Ohio Not For Profit Corporation and a 501 (c) (3) qualified public charity. Contributions are tax deductible.

Executive Editor: Robert J. Murphy

Illustration & Book Design: Elizabeth H. Murphy
www.illusionstudios.net

Typeset in Adobe Garamond Pro & BonJovi
ISBN 978-1-962847-29-2
Library of Congress Control Number: 2025940953

GRATITUDE

Thanks to Allan Appel, Allen Bergson, Deena Metzger, Elizabeth and Robert Murphy, Deborah Offenbacher, Madelaine Santner, Ron Susser, Mark Weiss, Eileen Wiseman, and Steve Zeitlin: their generosity, steadfastness, editorial discernment, and technical support were the blessing that helped sustain the writing of this book.

for Deena Metzger and Mark Weiss

Would like to see a large Yiddish theater [because] the production [of Joseph Lateiner's play *The Apostate*] may after all suffer from the small cast and inadequate rehearsal. Also, would like to know Yiddish literature, which is obviously characterized by an uninterrupted tradition of national struggle that determines every work.
　　—Kafka, *Diaries,* October 8, 1911

The [Yiddish] actors by their presence always convince me to my horror that most of what I've written about them until now is false. It is false because I write about them with steadfast love (even now, as I write it down, this too becomes false) but varying ability, and the varying ability does not hit off the real actors loudly and correctly but loses itself dully in this love that will never be satisfied with the ability and therefore thinks it is protecting the actors by preventing this ability from exercising itself.
　　—Kafka, *Diaries,* October 23, 1911

I found [the letters to Felice] more gripping and absorbing than any literary work I have read for years past. They belong among those singular memoirs, autobiographies, collections of letters from which Kafka himself drew sustenance. He himself, with reverence his loftiest feature, had no qualms about reading, over and over again, the letters of Kleist, of Flaubert, of Hebbel.... In the face of life's horror—luckily most people notice it only on occasion, but a few whom inner voices appoint are always conscious of it—there is only one comfort: its alignment with the horror experienced by previous witnesses.
　　—Elias Canetti, *Kafka's Other Trial: the Letters to Felice*

Author's Note

Many of the poems and prose pieces that follow are collaged texts, combining fragments of Kafka with imaginative and documentary writing. My key documentary sources include Kafka's *Diaries*, Max Brod's *Franz Kafka: A Biography*, Ernst Pawel's *Franz Kafka: The Nightmare of Reason*, and Reiner Stach's *Kafka: The Decisive Years* and *Kafka: The Years of Insight*. This work is a midrash—a speculative narrative and commentary—written from the perspectives of Kafka, some of the people in his life (Max Brod, Yitzkhok Leyvi, Dora Diamont, Kafka's father Hermann) and a variety of fictional characters (participants at a fictional Kafka conference, as well as a Yiddish folksinger/independent scholar, a Yiddish actor, and a refugee-informant). Sources of the collaged texts are cited in the Source Notes.

TABLE of CONTENTS

I. HIS ROOM

II. BOTCHED REVELATIONS

III. ASTRAY

IV. KAFKA: THE BUREAUCRAT AS ARTIST
PROCEEDINGS OF THE CONFERENCE

V. DISAPPEARING ACTS

VI. THE KAFKAN SENTENCE

APPENDIX TO THE PROCEEDINGS
OF THE KAFKA CONFERENCE

KAFKA'S AX

I. HIS ROOM

My preoccupation with portraying my dreamlike inner life has relegated everything else to a secondary position; other interests have shrunk in a most dreadful fashion, and never cease to shrink. Nothing else can ever make me happy. But it is impossible to calculate how much strength I have for this portrayal. It may have already vanished forever; it may come back to me once again, but the circumstances under which I live are not favorable to it.

—Kafka, *Diaries*, August 6, 1914

1. A Dry Eye in the House

After his days
at the office, he set out
for the sea, the one he wrote
about to Oskar Pollak,
whose lips he wanted

to keep always close
to his ear: "What we need
are books that hit us
like a misfortune, a book
must be the ax for the frozen

sea within us." A stiff
discipline carried him
across the frozen time:
a light snack, reading,
a nap, a walk, dinner

with parents, by ten o'clock
he resumed demolition
of the blinding
horizonless screen of ice
he had to break through

with the written word, yet he
knew the peculiar character
of their Germanjewishczech
existence couldn't be
rendered as tragedy,

it compelled a cold kind
of writing, pure
as a port-mortem report,
a scrutiny that let no one
escape into catharsis.

2. A Stray

Ax, an act and a thing
of beauty, a tool
men use to heat
their rooms on cold
nights, a honed
head on a curved
handle.

In pursuit of
it, he goes back
to the old ghetto
of Prague with
its bookstalls and
bordellos.

*

This evening I saw a woman in a fur
cap and stole with a pup
on a leash, training him where
to relieve himself with the command, Get busy.

Not four months old, and already a word
from his mistress is enough
to set the little dog running
in tight circles.

*

It comes out in heated
moments, he sighs, he covers
his eyes with his hands, his arms
drop to his sides, his tongue rears up
in his mouth and spews out Yiddish
curses that belong to his ghetto

past, *Zolstu zayn a lomp,*
you should be a lamp, *hengen*
bay tog, brenen bay nakht,
hang by day, burn by night,
un oysgeyn in der fri, and
extinguished in the morning.

He's turned his father's curse
into a way of life, but every Jew
in a blue suit carries the ghetto
through the streets of Prague.
Slum clearance never finished it
off. A remnant remains of

the vaulted archways and crooked
streets that haven't changed
since the days they sprang up
helter-skelter: now a poor
quarter where meat and milk
keep company, it still goes under

its medieval name: Josephstadt.
Here he returns from the trance
of the normal life—in the *Judengassen,*
filthy and narrow, and largely
unsignposted, he's free to go
off where his nose takes him.

*

Not free not to
repeat his daily round

between the office
and his room in his parents' house

in the Altstädter Ring—
loses track of him-

self and time in alleys
where he sniffs, pricks

up his ears to listen—all
quiet—his hearing extends

deeper into the night—someone
walking fast—something rattles

in the room he carries
inside him—a mirror

not quite firmly fastened
to the wall.

3. THE BLACK LETTERS

Committed to the madhouse
where he was stripped
of every purpose but autobiographical inquiry, many
times a day he walked to the
sink, let the water run to
scalding, wash your hands.

To be ready at every moment
to stain the sheets with black
letters that traverse the distance
between his fantasies
and the purity he aims at.

*

A waste of days, a sin
against the fathers, unending
repetition of the same,
a vocation that granted him
the privilege of leading
his own particular life,
half a life, a break
in the chain of
generations, a shame,
a demand that he travel
in the dark between contradictions, an
expense of spirit, lusting after
the impossible, his only way
out of mother Prague.

*

He dreamt of ending
his days in Palestine
but went back and forth
between desk and sink—

What have I in common
with the Jews? I
have hardly anything
in common with myself.

4. Repititon of the Same

He loved the smell
of their bindings, the feel
of their covers—books
on display elated him.

After work he dropped in
to visit the new arrivals
and pick one whose uncut
pages he took home to bed.

There he was comforted by
any writer in whom he
recognized this own torments
and ecstasies as he read

his letters and diaries,
the book falls from his hands and
he is in it, climbing
out of the city until he

realizes he is making no
progress but simply
running around in his own
labyrinth, more excited,

more confused than before.

*

And he would think
of his father—how he popped
into the synagogue to reel
off a few quick prayers
                    to whatever
still adhered to their ancestral
metaphors after a life

of keeping up his inventory of dry
goods and tearing down
the throne on which the absolute
Name sat among starry
messengers

his father went on repeating the square black
letters on the page
                    without sensing the white
fire of the space around them, dancing

letters of the Invisible that warmed
the shivering lives of his shtetl grandfathers.

Little Jews, they were masters of burrowing
through the plain sense of the text
and holing up in the elusiveness
of the Torah. Only they
could say, We
are the People of the Book.

*

He imagined they came away
from the portion of the week
feeling cleansed, he fouled
their memory, wondering if they also failed
to rein in the lust—gnawing
at him night and day, hounding him
through alleys that opened
onto funnel-shaped interior courtyards.

*

He retraces his steps
back to his father's house
to be questioned by his own right
hand, which keeps strict accounts
in letters, notebooks, diaries—

What have you done
with your gift of sex?

5. His Room

It's too small
for his necessities:

a bed, a chair, a mirror, a wardrobe,
a small, dark brown desk,
a few books, a lot of
notebooks strewn about.

Spare to the point of austerity.
No room to move around.
No object drags the mind
out of its withdrawal
from the senses, except
two noisy reproductions, amulets
against the noises of the house.

*

A copy of Hans Thoma's "Ploughman"
hangs over his desk, a tiny figure
laboring at the edge of the sea
under four dark clouds

in a baroque sky, performing
the gospel according to Doré,
announcing the Kingdom with a fanfare
of four blasts of light.

On the wall to his right, a yellowing
plaster cast of a maenad, brandishing
the dismembered leg of a bull.

After every humiliation,
he sits down in
the mind of the room.

*

His sister Elli is pregnant. Never again
does he want to feel such envy.

He is, after all, his father's son,
doomed by his belief

that the greatest thing in life is to
marry, have children.

Not a day goes by when he doesn't write
to his fiancée, to prove

he is unfit for marriage.
She remains steadfast

in her refusal to understand:
he will never bring a child

to his father's table.
In warring against mortality,

his brother-in-law carries a weapon
between his legs.

He has only a pencil.

*

The sky is verbose, the sea
reflects the radiance of heaven,
only the ploughman is mute,
his head bent under Adam's curse.

His own bent beneath the ploughman's.

*

And he writes under the sign
of the raving woman, she

wears snakes and an ivy wreath,
fierce bulls fall to the ground

before her female hands
which tear them to pieces

and threaten him with the raw
meat she devours.

*

Sitting at the desk over the white
page, he converts the narrow room
into the strait gate
through which he meets the gaze
that at every moment writes the Last
Judgment of the life
he fails to live outside his room.

6. The Card Players

Savage beings
who could not be appeased

they spoke only to set the air in motion

their words were small
shapes amid formless clamor.

The rocket of Father's voice
blasting over the women's talk
exploded in laughter, igniting
idiotic giggling

shrapnel of sense
ripped into me from across the hall

a lull

I tensed up, waiting

for the next outburst

and came up against the wall
of Mother's whispered Yiddish

her words triply camouflaged.

*

Every night of her married life
she consented to his regime
of the card table.

She inducted us one by one

and later unconsciously played the part
of a beater in a hunt
flushing me out of hiding

until his grandson came along
to fill the place I'd left.

*

Words sometimes reached me
from the other room.

How rash
to believe I could therefore
reason with him.

I would break
into his play to prostrate
myself in argument

before I lost the capacity
to talk, even to think,
in his presence.

*

No use
throwing open the door in my nightrobe,
notebook in hand, trying
to plead my case.

7. THE STORYTELLER

Timid as I was, I couldn't get it
through my head not to
disturb the old bull taking his
pleasure with my mother and sisters.

From early on, I knew
I was the wrong one: masochistic
defiance was my habitual
stance, my stump
of aggression, my offense,
my way of ruining his good
time at the card table.

Yes, I exaggerate.
Yes, I'm too sensitive.
Yes, I loved and admired
my tall, broad-shouldered father,
a shining example of
hard work, endurance, devotion
to family, brute strength.

I dedicated my first book
to him, but when I tried
to hand it to him, he said,
Put it on my bedside table.

*

And I see
the bull taking wing, becoming
the swan, becoming the god
of the household, who carries off
any female he desires, changing
her into cow or queen.

I too get carried away—
by the lines of flight
I invent

*

The body remembers a small
mammal, flush with its triumph
over gravity,
standing up and beginning
to walk like a man, like
a little man—I believed
my mother would always
intercede.

*

When Father ran around
the table, grabbing at me,
shouting, I'll tear you apart
like a fish, I was really
torn apart: part of the child
knew nothing worse
would follow, and another
part remained alive
only by his leave.

*

I tell stories to set out
again
from the scene
where the vestigial
wings I was born with
were clipped
too soon

and to bear the phantom
pain
of it into the upper
air where I change
form and fly

over the head of my father.

*

I know what goes on
in his bedroom: he wrestles
with my book, the slow
narrative pace, the speed
of fear racing in all directions from the point
of impact, stress cracks in every
sentence, sentence by endless
sentence he becomes more
confused, frustrated, ashamed
that he can't understand my kind
of writing.

*

Oh, to be a fisherman
casting my net through whose holes
the little fish escape,
and the great carnivores can't bite
through the twine out of which I weave
the soft cage that captures them.
But my fishing expeditions never end
like that: shoals of fleeing fish abruptly
change direction, the light
flashes off innumerable silver-blue flanks,
comes and goes in frantic zigzags
as it's eaten piecemeal
by the jaws caught in the net.

8. In Lieu of Suicide

Agonies in bed. No way
out. Even Mother and Ottla
are in on it—they insist that I
spend my afternoons in the asbestos factory, minding
Father's business.

The only solution—throw
my suit on, rush to the Chain
Bridge, vault
over the railing, let myself sink
into the Vltava.

*

Same scene over and
over. Sentenced to death
by drowning. Jump

into the third person and narrate
the night—I, no, he
will want to live to tell the suicide tale.

*

In the hall between the two bedrooms
—his and his parents'—two eyes
entrap him in the mirror with the gilded frame—

smash it, scream, You've ruined me
forever! No, pluck his eyes out
of the glass, turn his gaze

onto the blank page, take up
his pencil—only a crane
could lift it now,

this girder of wrath
could be used to build
the vault of Hell.

*

Father's right. I
make an enemy of everyone,
speak to no one.
No, not I—he.

*

star bursts, bull's eyes, flashbacks'
impacts on
and off, thoughts
racing, no words
for it, memory
debris flooding by
too fast to be
remembered, a pile up,
seven years old and
plunging his fists into his
eyes, a twenty year old
bringing his lips close

to his friend's ear, a whorl-
pool sucking him
under, stop, can't
stop how long
will it take
him to drown

*

Sick of my alibis. Apologize
and die. Father, Felice, I
won't keep you
waiting for a kind word
from me any longer, I will pass into
oblivion through the river running softly
below my window—I will be he, will
be gone.

*

And be denied a place in the Jewish
cemetery? Or buried apart from
the others? His head against the stone wall.
Is his shame in living greater than
the shame of suicide?

*

Half-cocked pronouncements come
back, like the one he wrote
to Oskar years ago—
I'm an atheist who believes
God doesn't want me to write.

Showing off his wit,
carrying defiance up to the empty
heavens, preening to keep Oskar's pen
engaged in their correspondence.

Toward dawn, he sees he got it
wrong: the God he doesn't believe in
commands me to write.

*

Lord—if I may
address You as the faithful do—
let me continue
to serve you, help me
not do the thing
I would do, let me
only lie here and wait.

9. Toward Dawn

a butcher knife in the air
carving slices out of my side

a wild squealing
in the walls

dread of falling
asleep, dread
of staying awake

*

For all things outside the physical
world our language is only a sort of
adumbration, angels
speak to us, Maimonides writes, in high

frequencies we register as
sensations no words for this
that I feel I can describe
it only as it speaks through

the body—where my stomach
should be, a hole
shaped like an egg
expands, its internal surface

a band of steel that presses against
my still living tissue, obstructs

the movement of my dia-
phragm, threatens

to suffocate me, unless
I jump up, forget
sleep, gasp
for air.

*

Every person is given a room where
he may remain faithful
to what he desires. For me,
it's the bedroom where
I dream subterranean corridors,
spiraling staircases, roads buried
in snow, deserts, trackless
wastes over which I go on
sending determined messengers.

*

You long to cross oceanic
distances, the ancient world beckons
with its shipwrecks and resurrections,

masts and crosses float by within
easy reach, but if you clung to them,
you would have to forsake

the formlessness of your journey,
you would lose your chance
to find the one thing needful: an image

of your fate that doesn't
betray the circumstances and
scale of your creaturely life,

to remain loyal to the little
people in whose midst you belong
and to release the frail song

of your existence, you will
have to confine yourself
to the piping of

mice, driving you
to the world hidden
inside your four walls.

*

Stuck between fear and desire, shaking
with fatigue, ready
to give up, you tell yourself,

Reverse direction, determined messengers
are trying to reach you, listen
and let them take you

to the hiding place
where safety and dread meet in one
tight passage.

10. His Daily Practice

He returns after
his days to his private
fiction
that his improvisations are mere
entries in a diary, he tricks
whatever it is that makes his pencil
too heavy to lift.

There between the draft of a letter
to his fiancée and a note
that he spent yesterday at court,
the death-ship of a medieval hunter
sails into a tiny harbor and docks
where only fishing boats and two
ocean-going steamers usually call.

Now it's too late to stop the Hunter
Gracchus from telling his story
to the Burgomaster of Riva, then
lying down on his bier,
he travels through all the seas
of the earth, searching in vain
for the gate to the other world,
a prey to stupid imaginations.

*

There he returns: to live

in the promise
of happiness he will never
renounce

while flaying
hope that clings

to the things
begun:

carpentry, Zionism, anti-
Zionism, gardening, Germanics,
Hebrew, piano, marriage,
an apartment of his own.

All broken off.

In the late afternoon he goes back
to sleep: to dream and wake up
in the writing. There he returns
to the starting-point of possibility,
the place where he abandons repetition
and lets his formlessness go
in search of his desire, the one
from which he takes flight in dreams,
from which his writing takes form.

*

In his dream, he finds
a pillowcase filled with old things—
silver candlesticks, gold rings,
a code written on pieces

of parchment—he takes it up
but doesn't know what to do
with it. He's afraid
that if he drops this bundle,
he will float off and never
return. In his dream,
he stands at the edge
of every group, he's in
a summer camp, a counselor
of sorts, but he alone
is not permitted to escort
a child across the hillside
where he has no part
of the action, it's almost beyond
him to walk from one place
to another, to adhere
to the ground with the bottom
of his feet, like everybody else—
he wants to ask the others
if he can put down the bundle
but somehow he has lost
the capacity to speak
and can only write out his question
on little conversation slips,
in this way an answer
is forced upon him: to write,
he must lay down the
bundle for brief periods
and look into it with a free hand
that destroys his inability
to make use of his great power.

*

Little walking stick, seeing-
eye cane, wand of my travels—
don't slip from my hand
if I get carried away like this—

without reverence I'd be
lost, couldn't cast off
the fear that binds me
to my father's warehouse and keeps me
stumbling and blind in the world
of prayer, oh pencil!

be my diviner's rod,
lead me across the dry
plain, a little farther

and I shall yet find my hand
trembling in the presence
of running ground-
water.

*

And it happens past
one a.m. that the silence in the room
spreads through the whole
house and opens
onto the Great Plains where absence
is transformed into an image
of what he yearns for.

If one were only an Indian,
instantly alert, and on a racing horse, leaning
against the wind, quivering
over the quivering ground,
until one shed one's spurs,
for no spurs were needed,
threw away the reins,
for no reins were needed,
and hardly saw that the land
before him was smoothly shorn heath
when horse's neck and head would already
be gone.

II. BOTCHED REVELATIONS

Among the expedients taken by the young [Jews] of Prague to escape the city that offered them no hope for the future, writing enjoyed a surprising pre-eminence. Thus there was nothing very original about Kafka's flight into literature; it was remarkable only for its extraordinary precocity and all-encompassing character, which transformed it little by little from a quest for escape into a quest for the absolute.... Dedicated from an early age to this salvation through writing for which he was to strive all his life, he derived much less joy than suffering from the exercise of his talents. "You see," he wrote to a friend [Oskar Pollak], "this misery has been on my back from early on...," for his writing, directed essentially against his father's tyranny and the narrowness of his environment, was anything but an innocent game. It was a dangerous offensive weapon, the use of which brought with it a profound sense of guilt....

Tormented by what he felt to be the profound aggressiveness of writing in general and his own writing in particular, of whose hidden violence he was perhaps more aware than anyone else, and fearing that he might be influenced by his models to the point of not always distinguishing what he took from others and what was truly his own (he spoke ironically of his writings as a mixture of things "coming from myself and others"),... writing soon became the main source of his anguish. It frightened him in two ways: as a dangerous weapon against society, which not without reason he was afraid of wielding too well; and as property, created by others and belonging to others, which he was in constant danger of robbing.

—Marthe Robert, *As Lonely as Franz Kafka*

11. In His Father's Warehouse

His memory was bad. He relied on me and his diary to keep his head anchored to his feet. He spent much of his time at sea, in the exercise of his imagination: in reading and reverie; in marking passages and making notes; in the company of storytellers.

In Prague, he dreamed continually of leaving Prague; to him, all of Prague was a tightrope stretched between two extremes, with no middle. He could see a middle ground from the place where he hovered in mid-air, but he couldn't reach it without losing his balance. Franz wished to be numbered among ordinary men, but the demands of the art he practiced were absolute. He tried to run from the mad bachelor life he lived, but how do you run with an abyss at your feet and only a single strand of rope to hold you aloft? He was incapable of sacrificing writing to the god of his father, the householder, and he couldn't sacrifice an ordinary life for the sake of writing. With supreme detachment, he tracked his failure to do the impossible, and turned his ongoing defeat in Prague to the advantage of the artist. I am not alone in thinking that his writings are among the decisive literary achievements of our age, but this is probably more amazing to me than anyone else because I saw, up close, out of what wretched materials he created the myth of homelessness that haunts the imagination and illuminates the self-understanding of our time. He supplied us with a name—his name—for the weird situation—our situation—where helpless supplicants encounter power that is brutal, elusive and indifferent, and we lose our bearings. If one of the ends of the tightrope was held in an obscure realm of the absolute, the other ended in the warehouse where Franz tried to serve his father, the merchant of fancy goods, who never stopped taking inventory of his son's faults. In this regard, the son took after his father: picking himself apart was a way of life for him, if for no other reason than to beat his father at his game and render the latter's judgment secondary to his own. In this, too, he judged himself a failure.

Once when we were talking in his room, his father threw open the door and said in his booming voice, "So you won't go to the factory? Your scribbling is more important than helping your father, whose workdays never end? What is your scribbling anyway? Mental masturbation, as far as I can see." His father was a coarse man, he was usually callous, but outrage at his son's acts of defection made him cruel. Franz sank deeper into his chair, his head bowed, his left hand shading his eyes. Didn't say a word. The father was left standing in the doorway, fuming, saw he would get nothing from his son, and walked away, leaving the door open behind him. Franz sat there, frozen.

In how many conversations did I not try to make clear to my friend that he overestimated his father, that he was too sensitive, that it is stupid to despise oneself. Useless. The flood of arguments that Franz produced, when he didn't shroud himself in silence, could shatter and repel me, if only for a moment. In later years, he hardly spoke to his father, yet he suffered from the distance he put between them. The shadow his father cast over his life lengthened the farther he tried to get away from him. I couldn't keep myself from posing the obvious question, with a sober arrogance whose justification was that I clearly saw what was in his best interest: "What do you need him for?" Or, better put, "Why can't you break away from him?" Franz got tired of my raising the subject, his neck stiffened, he couldn't move his head at all, and he shut his eyes.

Sometimes, accompanied by me, he would visit his father's warehouse on the ground floor of the Kinski Palace. "Not again," I would say. "Yes, again. There was a big delivery this afternoon. Mother spoke to me about Father's weak heart. Ottla and Elli are coming in, and so am I." This, despite the fact that his father dressed him down in front of family and staff. One time, as Franz and I walked in, he shouted, "My son the navel-gazer, and his friend the star-gazer!" Franz simply walked to the nearest crate, removed the packing slips, and started to check that nothing was missing. I began to stock shelves. I remember quantities of warm slippers, ornamental combs, buttons and buckles, hooks-and-eyes, photo frames, grommets, bootlaces, notions and novelties, all of it had to be picked through to fill the new orders, packed up again and shipped to retailers in the surrounding villages. Franz worked diligently alongside his family in another vain attempt to help his father, or at least show his good will, and by his small useful gesture win a friendly glance or a word of recognition.

We put in a good two hours of work. The job was still unfinished, but Franz stopped abruptly, walked to the door and bade his father good-night. "Ach, Frank," his father called from across the warehouse, "Leaving so soon? A little physical labor tired you out?" Then he bellowed, "You're hopeless, Frank, you're an airhead, a *luftmentsh*."

Franz, struck down by the truth of it, grabbed hold of the doorknob and waited for his vertigo to pass. Carefully, he stepped out into the street, and, walking carefully on the longitudinal cracks in the pavement, he made his way across the great distance that now separated him from his bed. He couldn't measure himself against his father without feeling small and impotent. He loved and admired his father's virtues—his strength, discipline, tenacity, self-satisfaction, and, until recently, his robust health. He himself was peculiarly unsuited to stand up to life in the ordinary way, as his father did, drawing strength from the ground on which he stood.

I walked beside my friend, heavy-hearted as I watched his all-too-deliberate footsteps marking off the line he had to walk in order to get safely back to his room. I asked, "Why do you bother?" "I need to improve my memory for certain kinds of details." "I thought whatever details you need come to you while writing." "Yes, but only if I'm totally in the world I'm writing." "What does this have to do with working for your father?" "I'm talking about notions and novelties." "You're pulling my leg." "Not at all. Don't you remember how I outfitted the warder Franz, who arrested K.? He wore a tight-fitting black suit, furnished with all sorts of pleats, pockets, buckles and buttons, as well as a belt, you can't tell what purpose this suit actually served, but it works, it looks eminently practical."

"No, Franz, your clowning around doesn't work. Your father calls you hopeless, you tell me you're hopeless, but you're not hopeless enough. When will you realize that you'll never get what you want from him?"

On the rare occasions in my life when I've been in despair, I've felt dulled, empty-headed. Desperation had the opposite effect on Kafka, it enhanced his agility; this allowed him to jump out of my reach, just when I thought I had him cornered.

"Perhaps I need more shots of ill-treatment to inoculate me against guilt, so that I can go in my own direction without being paralyzed by my obligation to him."

"Isn't it enough that you live by his rules? Every morning you dress in a business suit and march yourself off to an office you hate, in lockstep with his daily routine. It's killing you."

"No, it's saving me, and if it incidentally satisfies him, so much the better. I could never write for a living, like you. But I can't hope that he will ever understand—he sees only the unhappiness of my days, not the writing I do after everyone goes to sleep."

We had discussed his separation of writing and livelihood *ad nauseum,* but he continued to throw it up to me, as though each time it came up was the first, as though I too would never understand it. Yet how well I knew his need to shelter writing from the world. Writing, for Kafka, was too uncertain, too dependent on conditions over which he had no control, it was too agonizingly slow a process. He couldn't let anyone near it, much less a boss. In *The Castle,* he writes that official decisions were shy as maidens; this was true of himself in his only sphere of power: writing. If he had put it out for hire, it would have had to submit to a boss's taste and the hands of his clock; the thing that mattered most to Kafka— the purity of his prose—would have been violated.

He was so entirely himself in every utterance that you could not reflect back to him the hole he was digging for himself without sounding in your own ears like a good-natured simpleton telling one of God's prophets to relax. Yet if not for me, he would have gone without human companionship. Although he loved purity above all else, he also craved the gratifications of ordinary life with its small pleasures and comforts. So I pushed past my occasional sense that I was unfit for the task—there was no one else—and took on my friend's penchant for self-torment. Didn't Augustine also love the circus? For someone who didn't personally know Kafka or who has never been sufficiently intimate with a great poet or artist to understand that a singular personality like Kafka's can contain a multitude of warring selves, it might seem that his contradictions are mine, that my bonhomie violates my view that he was on the path to holiness. But I witnessed how he was. At every point, Kafka arrived at a cross-roads, which didn't offer a way forward so much as a slightly altered position from which to take stock of his impasse. His asceticism admitted no compromise: he took his meals of nuts and yogurt alone, he chewed every bite exactly twelve times; at the same time, he still wanted to partake of the common banquet of life. A spiritual genius is, after all, a human being, and in his need to go on vacation and waste time in beer gardens we met as equals. In the warmth of our friendship he found respite from his loneliness. And he depended on me to contend with him.

"You say you're not fulfilling your obligation to your father. I don't know what you mean. What obligation?"

"To honor him."

"How can you honor a father who ill-treats you?"

"Exactly. It doesn't feel humanly possible. But the Fifth Commandment isn't withdrawn just because a father doesn't understand or even notice his son. The Ten Commandments is the one text in which the Absolute addresses us directly: it dispenses with the forty-nine levels of meaning that elsewhere veil God-language and speaks the absolute word—No. In this No, the distance between heaven and earth becomes evident. For every person, there is at least one Commandment that is quite beyond reach, it is thanks to this Commandment that a person's place in the world becomes real to him as a site of spiritual battle."

40

The aura of holiness that I often felt in Kafka's presence dissolved time and place, we might have been walking through the winding alleys of Safed in the days of Isaac Luria or in the forest near Hanipol where the rebbe Zusya used to go to pray.

"Of course working in my father's warehouse gets me nowhere with him, this is merely the act, the ritual act, if you like, that accompanies my struggle: my ongoing effort to feel the weight of his life, not only how it weighs me down, but—this is the heart of the Commandment—how it weighs him down. Didn't you hear him groan under the weight of today's delivery? Those groans were made heavier by a lifetime of hard labor. For years he had sores on his legs because his winter clothes were too thin; he often went hungry; when he was ten, he had to leave the *kheder* and push a handcart around in the nearby villages, and in winter, too. He started with nothing, and look what he accomplished. I should be grateful to him, but I hate him for constantly beating his hands together and bragging about the hardship of his life. He did it at supper when I was little, and he does it now. He says to Mother, as if I weren't there, 'Go tell these children how I grew up! Nobody knows anything about it! Nobody else has been through it! And what's more, nobody knows how easy his life is! This son of mine does nothing but complain—he has it too good!' Every year at Passover, he blesses the bitter herbs and says, 'How are my kids supposed to remember the crushing labor of the Israelites three thousand years ago when they can't remember the labor of their own father?' Max, he's right. I should ask to hear his stories, I should honor him for what he went through—the filth and self-denial of assimilation, which he can't permit himself to realize is a dead-end. And because I know this and he doesn't, I am all the more responsible to shore up his life of toil by honoring him. The word honor in Hebrew, *koved*, also means weight. We are commanded to recognize the weight of our father's suffering because it allows us to understand his way with us."

The revelation that Franz was learning Hebrew stunned me. This making a big secret of everything—there was something very great about it, but also something evil. I could not—I didn't want to—keep my hurt and anger out of my voice when I confronted him.

"It would have given me such pleasure to know that you're studying Hebrew—why did you keep it from me?"

"Why does anyone keep things to himself until he is ready to bring them out? Every step I take, even in the most basic things, especially in the most basic things, comes after prolonged hesitation, and involves the greatest difficulties. For me, the true way is along a rope that is not spanned high in the air, but only just above the ground. It seems intended more to cause stumbling than to be walked along."

12. The Broken Tablets

I had long cherished the desire to see a book of my friend's in print. Kafka's attitude toward this wish of mine was divided—he wanted to, and again he didn't want to. I prodded him until he handed over a few specimens of his writing, and I took them to Leipzig. There, I showed them to Kurt Wolff and Ernst Rowohlt, who immediately offered me a contract to bring back to Kafka. Those were happy days!

But then I returned to Prague. Kafka received the news of his success as if it were a blow to the skull. His diary is a witness to the resistance he put up against me, but it didn't help him in the least. I refused to join him in betraying the gift he had been given. I stood over him like a rod, and drove him and forced him, not directly, but again and again by new means and new tricks. Every strategy I used had a single aim: he had to set to work and choose those short prose pieces that he considered ready for publication from the wealth of his manuscripts, that is to say, his diaries. He didn't separate the chronicle he kept of his days from sketches, drafts of stories, and unclassifiable texts, speculations, self-analysis, strings of images, meditations on writing and the true way to redemption. His notebooks were the garden where he kept his green edge alive; to cut out and remove what he grew from the private sphere of his gardening—he was always an avid gardener—meant opening his green zone to potential destruction. As a fellow Jew, I understood his fear of the world and wanted to shelter him, but I believed he would not thrive unless he left the enclosure of the quarto-sized notebooks for the one thing no writer can do for himself: be his audience. "The book is written, at most it needs a little polishing. You just have to sit down and pull yourself together. If you like, I'll sit with you while you figure out the final selection."

"I'm sorry to have to inform you, Max, that the problem is altogether different than what you imagine."

It was as if he'd slapped me; he spoke only officialese with me when he was stung or anxious. It was hardly my purpose to provoke him—why couldn't he hold onto that? I, too, had to keep a tight rein on my feelings. I wasn't about to let him succeed in keeping me at bay and destroying any prospect of publishing his stories.

"In the act of writing, you yourself must realize—"

He cut me short. "No, it's not a matter of applying willpower to some technical difficulties. The angel that grabs me by the collar, drags me to the mountain top where things are written in stone, sustains me only to a certain point. I am granted as much as three-quarters of what was to have been made known to me, then the angel hurls me back down to the desert, where I am abandoned. What can I do with these botched revelations? These things can't be filled in and smoothed over the way you patch a cracked wall. Moses never considered getting down on his hands and knees, gathering up the shards of the broken tablets, and gluing them together. He needed a second chance on the mountain top. There's only one thing I can do: wait. Wait without any certainty that I will be given a second chance."

We were strolling along the Vlatava, on the outskirts of the city. With a sweeping gesture, I motioned for Franz to sit down on a bench overlooking the river, I opened my briefcase, rifled through my file of specimen texts, and read the piece that I pulled up at random, "Children along a Country Road." Franz grimaced as I began reading, then his brow smoothed, his taut lips parted, I'd caught him in his own net.

As I read, my tongue and breath felt a sweetness I have never experienced anywhere else. That language! It's like looking into the waters of the Aegean, delighting in the transparency of a nearly colorless element that allows you to see what swims and crawls at depths that in other seas are unfathomable. It's impossible for me to say how the man who lives in such close proximity to me achieves the peculiar quality of the Kafkan sentence. Everything is serene, healthy and simple, yet this is the medium that reveals the disquiet, the perversity, the uncanny logic of our time with an accuracy that no mimicking of our agitated lives in agitated prose can match. In every sentence he writes, the cadences, the breaks, seem to follow mysterious laws; the little pauses between phrases have an architecture of their own; a melody is heard that has its roots in other material than that of this earth. He sings of being in the world from the purview of a man who remembers the expulsion from Paradise—not Adam and Eve's, but his own—from the time before he was born.

We were quiet after I finished reading Franz his story. I was close to tears, and I was certain that I had disarmed him with the proof he had put into my hands when he authorized me to represent him in Leipzig. Surely, he had to see this was perfection, the perfection of pure form that brought Flaubert to tears when he stood in front of the ruins of the Acropolis. The fact is, when Kafka heard his own work read aloud to an audience of friends, that is, when he became the auditor of his work through his own performance of it, it was clear he knew his greatness. His habitual reserve fell away; he laughed as freely as anyone else in the room. Kafka wrote impersonal prose that is saturated with his own personal attitude; its sublimity comes from the forces that dominated his creativeness and bound him to his ancestors, the previous witnesses of the horror and mystery in everyday life, all the way back to the Jewish prophets; in him their passion for truth and justice survives. He hurls at his auditors and readers the ugliness or beastliness of our pursuit of satisfaction, acceptance and security; he seeks the path that leads behind the decaying facade we call civilization; he stages his encounters with guilt, sex and power in a hidden room in a bank, a tenement attic, a village inn. He never forgets his father's business occupies a corner—a very large corner—of the Renaissance palace that dominates the Old Town Square.

"*Nu?*" Franz said, startling me with his use of one of his father's Yiddishisms.

I was back in his father's warehouse, but wanted to stay focused on my purpose—helping my friend.

"I confess I'm lost in admiration for your work."
"Lost, indeed."

He changed the subject, spoke of a certain Lily he had visited the previous night. I would win no concession from him that day.

A letter came from Leipzig, a most deferential letter in which Kurt Wolff reiterated his wish to publish anything that Dr. Kafka might care to send him. That's when he began to kick good and proper. He launched a counteroffensive on three fronts: he was technically incompetent as a writer; he was stranded in a desert, incapable of finishing what he had started; his deficiencies as a writer were a source of shame to him.

Kafka was an impeccable critic and he saw his faults more clearly than anyone. "My experiences," he said, "are always full of gaps, it's only single things that I grasp, things I stumble across in my empty existence."

"But you grasp those things to their very depths."

"Nonsense. There's never any question of completeness."

"Homer aimed at completeness, Flaubert aimed at completeness, but you see more clearly than anyone else—don't make that face, it's true—that we live in the time of broken tablets."

Kafka smiled his wry smile, and I felt encouraged to continue in this vein, to show him how deeply I received what he had to say, and to get him to have greater faith in my evaluation of his work. "Surely you realize that your work is unprecedented. You write about the break in tradition without belief in Zionism or progress or anything else that might save us, but unlike others who feel what a disaster it is to live without an indestructible realm of values permeating our affairs, you don't write as if the break in tradition can be undone by preserving its truth in a metaphor. Your response to this crisis is the most Jewish of any writer who has seriously confronted it, yet only a very few readers living today understand that. Because the Jewishness of our writing doesn't inhere in its positive content, but in its longing for community and the redemption of the world."

He looked at me with the fixed gaze that told me he had stopped listening. Ordinarily I would have desisted and walked alongside him in companionable silence, but I'd been struck by a new thought as I was defending Kafka's work against Kafka, a thought that might cut through the fog in which he lost his way, and I couldn't risk leaving it unsaid.

"Perhaps the negativity of your insight—the destructive force that marks your originality—is the very thing that makes it hard for you to work these pieces into a finished book."

"I appreciate your trying to understand my weakness, but your idealization of me keeps you from taking it in. The truth is more banal, more shameful than you imagine. I'm inadequate and lack discipline. I don't know punctuation, my spelling is atrocious, the thought of spending my nights poring over a dictionary to get my spelling right—"

"You just told me it's not a matter of willpower and technical difficulties. Franz, don't you see? In the space of three minutes you switch from one side of the argument to the other! Anyway, there's no need for you to worry about proofing your texts. Kurt Wolff would be happy to relieve you of the task."

"You've just proven what I've been saying—that I'm weak and indecisive. How can I finish a book if I can't sustain a consistent position from one minute to the next? My poor spelling and erratic punctuation are the least of my worries, although they are symptoms of my deficiency as a writer. And this holds me back."

"What are you referring to?"

"The extremely limited character of my work."

"The intensive life doesn't wish to record impressions," I said. I realized as soon as I said this that I'd made a mistake. Readers and auditors, baffled by one of his stories and at a loss for what to say about it, routinely told him, "That was intense." But I was trying to say something different, something substantive—that for the sake of his vision, he had thrown over the reigning aesthetic of realist art, which privileged the impression. But he took this as stereotyped praise, and rejected it.

"The intensive life floating in space, apart from the physical world, is what you get in case studies, not art. I live under a barrage of impressions that overwhelm me, pin me down at an immense distance from my inner life and from everything nearest to me. I take cover by going into a blur, into my own private trench, and I feel alive only when I go over the top, cross the battlefield, and write down what I hear and see."

All this while we had been taking our customary route from our offices. When we reached his parents' house on Niklas Street, he stopped, turned and brought out the most wounding argument he had been holding in reserve. He said that, in trying to carry out my orders, or rather suggestions, well-intentioned as they no doubt were, he had discovered that everything he had written thus far was bad; that trying to piece together old worthless fragments bound him to a futile task and kept him from letting these things drop away from him. He was living in great fear, he said, that it was already too late for him. Just when everything in him was ready for creative work, and such work would be a heaven-sent solution to his problems, a real coming-to-life, I had embroiled him in a salvage job. It was bad enough that he sometimes had to stay late at the office, and for the sake of a brief or report that his boss needed him to produce on a tight deadline, he had to rob a body capable of such happiness of a piece of its flesh, but that I should place my project as his impresario ahead of the complete freedom he needed to go on writing—that was intolerable.

I was speechless. In reacting to me as if I were a taskmaster like his father or his boss, as if my effort to have his work published were placing a barrier between him and his writing, he was taking leave of his senses, and disavowing everything that was the basis of our friendship. Independently of each other, we had each committed our lives to literature, and had found, in our mutual recognition and love, a deep-founded sheltering.

"Good-bye, Franz."

I didn't show up the next day at the Clock Tower where we used to meet every afternoon a little after two, after our shifts ended. Nor did I see him on the following day. On the third day after the attack on Niklas Street, he sent a messenger to my office with a two-word message: "It's finished."

We met at my parents' house that night to go over the final text. The amount of material that Franz deemed worthy of publication was incredibly small, which forced upon the publishers a compensatory format: they set *Meditation* in unusually large type. This design, intended as camouflage, served to bring out the innermost quality of Kafka's prose. The first edition, now rare, consisted of 800 numbered copies whose 99 pages of gigantic lettering resembled ancient votive tablets.

III. ASTRAY

Franz had already begun the conventional round of calls on relatives and acquaintances and even went to Hungary, to Arad, with F., to visit her sister. Franz and the conventions! It was a pitiful sight. At the same time he certainly made every effort to conform to the conventions that were held to be seemly. Another partner might, it is true, have freed him from this compulsion with a good hearty laugh. At the same time it is doubtful, too, whether Franz wold have wanted or accepted this freedom. Comically enough, the pair of them paid even me a formal call, on July 9, 1917—the sight of the two, both rather embarrassed, above all Franz, wearing an unaccustomed high stiff collar, had something moving in it, and at the same time, something horrible.

—Max Brod, *Franz Kafka: A Biography*

13. THIS DEADNESS

Restless. Walking it off on deserted
streets. I'm not so lost
in conversation with Max that a pair
of clacking heels and a shock of blond hair

don't hurl me toward the whore
trying to hook my eyes, her perfume
immerses me in a stream
of thought that ends in her bed.

Evil is whatever distracts.
Max passes her without
a sideward glance. I'm thrown
from one trance into another.

*

I hate meeting
the need I deaden by day
lurking in every doorway.

I'm not ready to face
the fear that keeps me
from sleeping.

Come upstairs,
sit with me,
Max.

*

The cell in which I serve
a life-sentence—a model inmate—
I will get no time off
for good behavior—what you see,
Max, is the behavior which you call
noble—it's a mirage,
the only thing real is the cell.

*

You slip in and out
of futility, and forget, when you're in,
what it was like to be out. Soon,
perhaps tonight, the key
will turn in the lock, the door will open,
invisible guests will come and
release you.

It's true that I sometimes stumble
into that other world where
I'm granted freedom
of movement—the prisoner's dream
of awakening 3000 miles from Siberia
warms him as he freezes to death,
and the mirage of language

surrounds him with the Sahara
where it grows lush—
an oasis rises out of the heat,
a promise of water
to the unfortunate
body in which I'm dying of thirst.

*

Ach, you metaphors! You are things
that make me despair of writing—
padded walls of the prisonhouse.
The moment all that geography escaped
from my mouth, I felt dead,

as if a board had come between the actual
feeling and the metaphors of my description.
I would rather die than give up
knowing this deadness: it's the touchstone
which frees me from the illusion of escape.

14. His Lateness

You know better than anyone that I arrive everywhere
late. No other trait of mine has so tested
our friendship. How many hours have you waited
at the Clock Tower, and felt hatred ticking
in your throat? No, don't deny it—hate
made your voice hoarse in greeting,
but your immediate forgiveness
always stretched across the length of my lateness
to embrace me.

Even to my situation as a Western Jew I came
late. A peculiar passion—cheeks trembling,
then wet—erased the oblivion
to which our parents condemned their parents'
Yiddishkeit. Leyvi's troupe
of Yiddish actors burst onto the stage of the Savoy
and once again clay from our river
was raised up by incantation into
a golem walking through Prague, disguised
as a woodcutter, ax in hand,
bringing news of our misfortune.

*

Belated reverence and dread
sprang out of the germ-seed
of Jewish identity lodged
in a few stories about the past
my mother couldn't help
telling when memory surfaced.

*

My mother remembers how after
her mother died of typhoid fever at an early age,
her grandmother refused to eat,
spoke to no one,
and when the year of mourning was up,
she went out walking and never returned,
her corpse was pulled out of the river.

And my mother remembers how after
her grandfather died she had to hold on
to the toes of the corpse and ask forgiveness
for whatever wrongs she may have done him—
a pious and learned man with a long white beard,
he bathed in the river every day, even in winter,
he had to chop a hole in the ice.

Amschel, in Hebrew I am named after him.

15. The Double

He is called Yitzkhok Leyvi in the company of the
Yiddish actors whom he leads through the capitals of Europe.
My father germanizes his name and calls him Isak Löwy, with
all the contempt that the merchant of fancy goods has for
a mass-produced article. Max, whose yearning he answers,
calls him Yitzkhak Levi, the Hebrew name recalls the high
status of his caste, which, since the days in Sinai, performed
ritual services and instructed the Israelites in sacred lore.
To me, he is a man of no fixed name, an actor who moves
freely up and down the social scale in the Yiddish plays he
puts on at the Café Savoy. An ex-yeshiva *bokher* who read
too many forbidden books (Shakespeare, Schiller, Byron),
he is no longer welcome at the court of his father's rebbe
in Warsaw. A Western Jew among the hasidim, an Eastern
Jew among the assimilated, whom he courts, he is, precisely,
nowhere—in exile from the exile of his sect and the diaspora
of the contending Jewish communities, movements, parties,
factions, splinter groups. His worldlessness qualifies him
as my guide. He became an actor to escape the ghetto and
transmit the folk spirit to the likes of me, incapable of being
touched by any belief that doesn't take shape as somebody's
experience. Through him, I acquire tears, in tears I discover
I have lost brothers in the East. He is, above all, a storyteller.
From him, rivers flow for my fish-like emotion.

He discovered the counterlife of performance at the
age of four or five when his cousin Khaskel stuck a big black
beard on top of his small blond goatee, turned his kaftan front
to back and acted the part of a peddler in the Purim play at
his *kheder*. From then on, he had no peace until he received

regular beatings from the *melamed* for leading the other boys astray: he cast them in skits he thought out and mounted whenever the *melamed* was away from the *kheder*. At the age of ten, he was told by a neighbor's boy that there was really such a thing as theater where people dressed up and acted and sang every night, not only on Purim. This knowledge filled him with longing: he went out of his way to pass the Grand Theater opposite the Town Hall. There, he gazed at the posters and felt he was going to burst. At fourteen, he fooled his parents into believing that he was sitting in the *besmedresh* over folios of Talmud and learning Scripture, but in fact he was stealing away night after night to watch operas and plays in Polish. In *The Huguenots*, a play by a Jew, he found "*Lekho Dodi,*" the hymn to the Bride of the Sabbath, recycled without the change of a single note into ballet music; he was shocked but understood that he had been given a passport to the realm of shadows in which he was caught up in the struggle to leave the ancient world. This was his first encounter with *a gilgul fun a nign*—a metempsychosis of a melody—the image used by Peretz in one of his stories to follow the circulation of a song from Jewish ritual through streets and alleys to the theater and back to life among the Jewish masses. Concretely, this showed him the way to drain the old music and liturgy of its sacred authority and transfer its aura to everyday life. He did not forget to buy a collar and a pair of cuffs for every performance, and to drop them in the Vistula on his way home.

The first Yiddish play he saw, *Baal Teshuvah*, was about a man who repents of wandering in alien gardens and returns to the rigor and sweetness of a Torah-true life. Seeing this play, he wept for joy; he knew that he too must serve in the temple of Jewish art. Now, in one city after another, he repeats the break with tradition; he walks around in European clothes like a spider before his parents' eyes, like a mourner at a wedding. On stage, he puts on a black beard and a kaftan, and brings home the tradition of the oppressed to Jews like myself, who only yesterday believed that we were the enlightened ones. We were raised to think that if we discarded the yarmulke and *sheytl* and identified with our roles in the world, we could live normal lives. We thought we could be like everyone we passed in the street, and remain Jews in our homes. In his theater, we become ourselves, sick with pride and anxiety and self-division; he acts out the impossibility that betraying one's parents and violating the laws of their world can lead to happiness.

16. IN THE MIDST OF YIDDISH

And Yiddish is everything,
the words, the wordless melodies
that Leyvi hums, this feeling

of intimacy with the Jewish actor,
the shapes in air that his hands evoke,
unrolling the Biblical layer

of ice between the water above
and the water below
and the gestures of greenhorns

carrying their seedy luggage
off the steamship from Ashkenaz
onto the Lower East Side,

you forget your disdain
of our grandmothers' jargon,
your fear of the ghetto

tongue dissolves, suddenly
you find yourself in the midst
of Yiddish, as it turns complaints

into prayers that hammer the vault
of heaven into place, you enter the now-time
where formlessness and creation are one.

17. To the Bath House

On the night-train into the countryside
towns into fields and a river
of light over mountains

its after-image goes on flowing along with
the broken things it carries past him
on the other side of the window

as if the world were water bearing the last
traces of its destructiveness at high
speed after a flood

to wash away impurity, to return
to the time before
creation, until

the slight thickenings in the darkness
and flickering of lanterns
along unseen

roads or candles in distant
windows finally become
monotonous

*

In great perplexity he drives off
the emptiness that is about to overtake
him, diving into a book
of legends of the Polish
Jews, he sails across time:

a few days' journey to the East
brings you to the river
Sambatyon where the lost
tribes graze their sheep
near Mt. Ararat, while
at a nearby inn, the rebbe
of Mezritsh hitches his gig
to his team of very good horses
and covers the distance to Berlin
in the time it takes to pour
a pitcher of water over
your hands and say the blessing
before the Sabbath meal.

*

In a village not ten
minutes away from his spa, men
still sat in a *shvitzbod*
quoting prices of dry goods
and pieces of Talmud

sweating muddy streets
out of their pores, pouring
buckets of ice water
over their heads
shock of the *shabes*

separating them
from their weeks.

*

He came among them
on a Friday
as they cleansed themselves,
he alone wrapped
his nakedness in the *shmates*
they used as towels.

Breasts of old men
with nipples like pinkies
sticking out of them—

as if to display
that they were the ones
who gave suck to this generation
of hasids, jumping
from the lowest tiers
to the highest.

The scent of pine
in the dry heat couldn't
blot out the stench
of the clothes
in the changing room.

*

Row upon row of bony
men with varicose veins
mingling with young ones

shapely as Assyrian archers—
the congregation of their bodies
in the steambath assured him
that he was in the right place
as if this were the natural-
health resort he most needed—
deviant thoughts—shame
brought him back to his senses—

how could he have imagined
that he might lose himself
in a room so primitive
that not even the air
had anything in common with the air
of his native town?

*

Yet he returned
from this expedition with something
he could make use of—

a proverb
that separated the Holy Word
from the marketplace:

Do not make the Torah your ax.
He grabbed hold of this
saying, went to town with it.

18. Do Not Make the Torah Your Ax

Dear Weltsch,

I feel your good will, and more than good will, your effort to understand what I'm doing with Yitzkhok Leyvi, when you call him my "informant," and it is true that I value the information he imparts to me. But this is a small piece of the truth, one, moreover, that falsifies the true nature of our relationship. We are friends, gates of experience that allow us to go beyond ourselves and look back at our lives with greater justice. Just as you reach beyond the prejudice of our tribe for a more balanced view of my friendship with the Yiddish actor. The humility, firmest union and earnest concern that I feel for my friends is as close as I've come to prayer. It is for the sake of this purity that I am drawn to him.

I hope you will understand why I've stopped coming to the Arco and spend my time at the Savoy or, as my father puts it, holed up with that little yid in my room, when I send you the story he improvised for me on one of our walks and then added to his repertoire of storytelling performances. He calls it "The Tale of the Bricklayer Rabbi," and presents its extravagant claims with utmost sobriety, the stance with which he ironically confronts us—Prague Jews who expect shmaltzy gesticulations from the *Ostjuden*. His irony lends a certain pathos to his abiding reverence for rabbinic storytelling; he narrates Jewish misfortune with a refusal to sink under it that no longer owes its buoyancy to faith but to something that grew up alongside it, the black humor of the folk tradition. Through him I draw close to a living Judaism. I hope Leyvi's rabbi turns up some night in one of my own stories. To feel that hope, even for a moment, makes it possible for me to enter the time of waiting in which my eastern brothers live with the lateness of the Messiah.

"In Zaleszczkyi, the village my father comes from, they used to say: "The best bricklayer of all the carpenters is the rabbi." It was also said: "He starves with the help of two professions."

"In a village of wooden houses, what kind of man becomes a bricklayer? The Bricklayer Rabbi, forbidden by the unwritten law to make a living by teaching the written one, prepared himself for the hour when the Messiah would come, even in Zaleszczkyi new housing would be ordered, so that all the cold creatures could take shelter. Then his great skill would be put to use.

"Years passed. He received at most two or three commissions a year, always from aristocrats living abroad. He realized that in his own lifetime his knowledge would never become practical. He turned to carpentry, only to find he had acquired a third noble calling, as the result of a misfortune. On the day he completed his apprenticeship, a ukase was issued that forbade Jews from leasing forests from the landed gentry and hiring peasants to cut down the trees and bring them to market, and this led to preventing Jews from having anything whatsoever to do with lumber.

"He spent the rest of his days chasing after a livelihood. In his hands any profane trade quickly became as unworldly as his original one, which he never ceased practicing, going to the Eternal Well to draw out new interpretations, generous helpings of Torah, which he cast into stories, so that they would not be entirely lost in this world.

"That storyteller, Franz, is my rabbi."

Yours Kafka

19. In Search of a Master

I wait for a long time before I catch a glimpse of the Master.
In his black Prince Albert coat, he comes toward me with arms
half spread and leads me down the corridor to his hotel room.
There, I try to show my humility, which I cannot feel,

by seeking out a ridiculous place for my hat;
I lay it down on a small wooden stand for lacing boots.
He keeps me from looking around by trying to hold me
with his gaze, but I push on with my prepared address:

"It's tempting to begin with an inventory of complaints,
as I would speak, for example, to my fiancée,
but you, I know, have no time for this, and want
to get at my character with a few broad strokes.

Allow me, then, to step out of character—or rather,
the character by which I'm known—and approach
my question with all the simplicity
and forcefulness that I can sometimes summon.

My happiness, my abilities, and every possibility
of my being useful will thrive if
I'm at the writing to which I cannot devote myself.
And here I have experienced states (not many)

that correspond to the clairvoyance you describe,
Dr. Steiner, I have dwelt completely in every idea,
but also filled every idea, and not only felt myself
at my boundary, but at the boundary of the human

in general, yet I cannot live by literature alone
because of family complications, and the slow maturing
of my work, the transports on which it depends
are erratic, and to have a place in the world

where men are breadwinners, I also must be one.
With a doctorate in Law, I have become an official
at an insurance agency, settling claims
between injured workers and the state. Outwardly,

I fulfill my duties—and who, lacking persistence,
could see these cases through?—while every unfulfilled
inner duty becomes a Fury hammering at my door.
If I have written something good at night,

I am afire the next day at the office, and bring
nothing to completion. The smallest good fortune
in one realm is a great misfortune in the other.
This back and forth continually becomes worse.

Anything I write is ruined in advance by the neglect
that all who depend on me must suffer if I write
or that I must endure if I don't fail them.
What can I hope for but a book that exhumes

the ruins which mark the course of the war along
the bondary between these never-to-be-reconciled aims?
And to these two endeavors shall I now add theosophy
as a third? Will I, already so unhappy a person,

be able to bring all three to completion?
This is what I have come to ask you, Herr Doktor,
for I have the presentiment that if you think me
capable of this, I really can take it upon myself."

Dr. Steiner listened attentively, nodded from time,
to time, at first a quiet head cold disturbed him,
his nose ran, he kept working his handkerchief
deep into his nose, one finger at each nostril.

20. In Bed

Just look at yourself.
I do little else.
What do you see?
An ape in formal attire.
You're a human impersonator?
Not when I write, I
face the direct gaze
that's my one virtue
and head
back into the fray where
I encounter myself,
but if I were to lie
side by side in bed
with a wife, I'd
be totally hemmed in.

*

What do you crave
in imagining yourself
an animal? In the body
of an ape or a mouse, I feel
a vestige of tenderness
for the creaturely life.

*

And what do you crave
in living? The repetition
on a page of my being
disbarred from family.

*

What have you gained
by your gift? As if
drifting to sleep, I
resume my night
watch, an image
floats by on a trackless
sea, the futility
of my striving ceases,
I follow the image across
the date line and
the latitudes of the known
world into the bed
of its metamorphosis,
a toothless father springs
erect and becomes a giant
delivering judgment, a son
wakes up to discover
that overnight he's turned
into a gigantic bug,
and the morning comes
and I'm in ecstasy.

*

Metaphor, you are the bucket
I ride through the jammed streets of the city below
my window, and over the bridge to the shore
where I go to draw water—but oh
how I long to dump the bucket
into the river and jump in

after it and be borne
by the current that flows
through the midst of the city.

*

And what would you find if you escaped
from Prague with your life? A day
in Marienbad with Felice.

*

The memory of it
a torment. Door
to door, keys on both
sides. Eyes other than
my own sought me.

*

No matter where
I go, I go nowhere.
Dread if I move
too far from her,
dread if I come
too close. No cure
for my kind of
motion sickness.

21. His Nausea

Langer's grown *peyes*, put on a wide-
brimmed black hat, and surrounded himself
with the scent of onions.
He eats scraps
of fish his rabbi first picks apart
with bare fingers, and ingests them
as if they were an infusion of
the spirit of God. Blatant superstition.
It leaves me wobbling. I feel
helpless, an outsider, a nothing that wants
to surrender to the roaring nothing
whose nothingness consists of its being
inconceivable. I envy Langer's self-
forgetfulness, feasting at the communal meal.

*

A man at peace with himself:
his stomach acts in accord with the Law
he lives by, he need not strive,
the operation of nature in him keeps him
pure: told he's eaten meat cooked in a dairy pot,
he simply vomits it up, and sits back
down to swallow his food with pleasure.

*

And my nausea?—has no
boundaries, it comes and goes as if
I were confined in a ship rolling
in heavy seas, as if the waters
were breaking on the walls around
me, every second thought
makes my gorge rise—if I don't
scrape the slab of butter off
my bread or don't refuse flesh
of the lamb on my plate, I sink
into the storm inside my stomach,
sickened by the waves, the sound
of roaring, the cracking of sense
and outward things, drowning
in images in which I encountered
myself without knowing it, I
hear a hoof tearing up the ground
where no ground was given to me—
it's me coming through the din
of my formlessness, me making
my presence known, rather trying to
make my hunger known and
at the same time keep it hidden
in the labyrinth of my intestines.

22. A Private Ritual

He proposed marriage to Felice by letter, lowered the blinds, lay down in the dark, shut his eyes, and waited.

Flight through the slum, chased by dogs. Crazy alleys, shuttered windows, squalid yards, sinister houses, barking. A desperate burst of speed, and he's there. In his office, writing a report that's due in the morning.

In this scene, Felice catches him in the act, pen in hand, he's trying to hide behind work.

Nothing to be done but see the thing through to the end. He drops his pen, his eyes, his head, they exchange places. She sits behind the desk, he puts on the high stiff collar that she hands him. He goes down on this right knee and asks for her hand to school him in marriage.

"Do you realize how late it is? Do you really think you can cancel five years of leading me on in three minutes?"

He begins a pleading apology—she cuts him short. She instructs him that he may not speak until she gives him permission.

"You live in a one-person time zone, only your nights count, your days are everyone else's nights. You don't care how long you keep people waiting. How can you possibly be with me in the future, let alone the present?"

As if his life depends on it, he asks what she expects of him. She screams that he is to be silent.

With a quiet ferocity that set his heart beating violently, she says, "I expect a proper proposal from you. Lay out for me what you have in mind."

He's breathless as he whispers something barely audible.

"Speak up. And give me details."

"When I'm gasping—really suffocating and begging for air—you stand up suddenly, as if at the last possible moment, as if you were hurting me only to show me this mercy."

"Go on."

"That's when I realize I'm not wearing pants."

"Hurry up, you're wasting my time."

"I call you *my beloved.* I say, *I love you enough to get rid of any qualities that disturb you. For you I will become another person. I ask you to punish me for having involved you in my torture.*"

"I've had enough of this, finish it off."

23. The Heightened Din

He wrote to his Intended: The forms
my decline takes are inconceivable—
writing letters in my parents' bedroom.

Leaden meaningless clouds drift by.

Sheer impotence.

*

To whom can he speak? Only
to someone who could hear a shriek
in his analysis of his condition,
but to such a listener above all
he could not speak.

*

Something like a breakdown.
His inner clock runs on at a demonic
pace, the outer one limps
at its usual speed, everything seems
over, yet he goes on, split
seconds ticking loudly in the dead
zone between the two worlds.

*

This latest collapse has brought him closer
to the last frontier, his hearing's grown more acute,
he picks up the *ts-ts-ts*
as of a mosquito buzzing about his ear

as if the sound of rebuke could spawn
a tiny guard whose tiny stinger sufficed
to carry him from the common banquet of life and
defend the Absolute against his assaults.

*

If his writing were only prayer and not art,
he would have calmed his incommensurable parts
in the namelessness of the Name,

but since his writing is prayer and also art,
he evokes a namelessness in which
the Name can't be in time and eternal and one.

*

Hallucinates bestiaries. Guilty
of committing them to paper, he won't give up
supplanting the world his father wanted
him to inherit with one that he needs to make
sufficient unto itself.

24. HIS FUTILITY

The work awaiting him is tremendous it can't be
done as long as he lives
under comfort's constant harassment.

The maid who forgets to
bring him his warm water in the morning
overturns his world.

The clock's irregular heartbeat the squeaking
pulley in the kitchen these things
make scratch marks on the soul drag it

out of its place beat it
flat and roll it
along the length of the skin's laughable irritability.

*

He hates writing's lack
of independence of the world—
its dependence on the maid
who tends the fire,
the cat warming itself by the stove,
the old man dozing in a patch
of sunlight on a bench.

These are independent
activities, ruled by their own laws.
Only writing is helpless, can't live
on its own, is a despair,
a joke.

25. A Little Phrase

I can't stand the sight of that
Greta, who is on duty all day
as a shop girl and at night
receives her clients in bed.

I won't say the sole reason for my hostility
(it surely isn't) is a little gesture the girl made
in all innocence to help me along (not worth mentioning)
and a trifling obscenity she uttered (not worth mentioning),
but at that instant I knew I would never forget it, I knew
it was just this repulsiveness that had drawn me
with such terrible power into the hotel—
this yearning for a small specific abomination,
some nasty smell, some sulphur, some hell.
This urge has in it something of the eternal
Jew, senselessly drawn to wander
through an obscene world.

*

First thrill of disgust—
in the countryside after a flood,
age six, bare feet sloshing through red clay,
Mother calling from the river bank, Come back! Debris
of houses and small boats swept away by wind and water, broken
things everywhere, the fulsome odor of decaying
fish all around me.

*

That little phrase! Resists
being written down, repeats
itself until the meaning's driven
out of it, goes on hammering like an awl
driven into my forehead, I feel my brains bursting
and running out of the hole.

26. Voice in the Head He Can't Escape

What is she who is she
daughter of a *shames* that doubles as a shoemaker
for this I wore out my legs to make something
of you when are you going to learn
that you are not a nobody Frank you want me
to stand by and watch you throw your life
away on this Julie do whatever you like
as far as I'm concerned you have a free hand to
destroy yourself.

What did she do put on a silk blouse
and let you see her tits
jiggle as she paraded in front of you these
Prague Jewesses are good at this sort of fishing
they wag their little finger and straightaway
you fall to your knees and ask for her hand
I can just imagine it please
Julie let me undo your buttons for
25,000 a year for the rest of your days
a good bargain yes marry her immediately
if not sooner in a week tomorrow today
I can't stop you I refuse
to stop you if it's so urgent you insist on ruining
whatever good Mother and I have done you
marry her.

Frank I'm sorry I know I shouldn't
talk to you like this I know you're a grown man
you live in a big city but still you can't think
of a better way to handle your problem
than to marry a girl who baits her hook with
her nipples haven't you heard of other possibilities
do I have to write down an address or can you
find your own way to the proper rooms
on Maiselgasse where you can rent it by the hour
if you're afraid I'll make it my business
to take you by the hand and pay some little actress
with garlic on her breath who doubles as a whore to
fuck you.

27. Make Him Go Away

By the light of a candle
I saw a strange
man sitting at a little table
in the center of the room,
broad and heavy he sat
in the dim light, his unbuttoned coat
made him appear even broader.

I leapt out of bed, reached
for my pen.

Undeniably, there is a certain joy
in being able to write
calmly down: "Suffocation
is inconceivably horrible." Of course
it is inconceivable—
That is why I have written nothing
down. When I looked up
from the page, the man was gone.

No sleeping after that.

28. Shocks

Rejected by sleep, I sleep alongside myself,
struggling with dreams in a twilight
state that's more exhausting than wakefulness.

This sleeplessness comes only
because I write, no matter how little
or badly, I am still made sensitive by these shocks

and feel toward evening and even more
with the first light between the blinds, the approaching
the imminent possibility of great moments

which would tear me open, make me capable
of anything, but in the general uproar
within me that I have no time to command,

they find no rest. In the end this uproar
is only a suppressed harmony, but left free
it would fill me completely, widen me, yet still fill me.

Now such a moment arouses only feeble hopes,
it does me harm, leaves me alarmed at the loss
of the pure, the true, the immutable.

I lack the capacity to hold the present mixture,
during the day the visible word helps me,
at night it cuts me to pieces unhindered.

29. Sounds in the Background

Belief in an absolute world, but
the angels that bar our return to Paradise
are put there by our lack
of self-knowledge, we don't see
our impatience carrying us away.

*

If I'm not mistaken, I'm coming closer
as though the spiritual battle were taking place
in a clearing somewhere in the woods,
I make my way into the woods, don't see
anything, and only through weakness
hasten out of the woods again.

Often when I'm leaving, I hear
or think I hear the clash
of weapons of those fighters, perhaps
their eyes seek me through the darkness,
but I know so little about them,
and that little is deceptive.

30. From the Book of Unfinished Stories

It became known that the rabbi was working
on a clay figure. A few disciples or neighbors
or strangers were always wandering up and
down the stairs and looking into his rooms,
in the attic they found a washtub with
a large lump of reddish clay on which the rabbi
had drawn the crude outline of a man. The liberty
the rabbi allowed everyone in his house
had spoiled them to such a degree, they
didn't hesitate to touch the clay and press
their fingers to their lips and taste
its bitterness at being separated from
insentient matter, laid out in a cold tub,
to spend frustrating nights with the rabbi,
kneaded and prodded and beaten to life.

*

Though the figure seemed
to be acquiring a human form,
the rabbi behaved like a madman.

*

He thrust his hands so violently
into the bucket beside him, water
splattered to the ceiling of the bare vault.

*

Passing one lip unceasingly over the other,
he plunged his hands into the clay
and began fashioning the joint of a finger—

bitter, bitter. How to solder these
fragments into a story that will sweep one along to its climax?

*

As the whole piece came
into view, he saw it was plainly
a figure in his own likeness
as a Jew and an artist—No!
He could never grant it a second
life outside his diary, not to
violate the abstract conception
of minutely observed gestures
through which he usually signed
his confession to the deaf world.

*

And if the thing were done
he'd have to see it
into print and commit
himself to promoting
it he'd have to
make the rounds to
have the bound copies
reviewed and the reviews
translated into sales Lord
help him he'd have to become a merchant

of the few drops of self-
knowledge that hadn't fallen
out of his cupped hands if
he brought the thing to completion.

*

Yet if he saw the thing through after all,
if he burst out of hiding in the guise
of the Rabbi of Prague and threw himself
at the public in a frank display of his greatness
and guilt as a golem-maker,

he would never be able to show his face
at the office, let alone the family
dinner table, even so he would never renounce
his excitement at writing it
to be spared his disgust at finishing it.

IV. KAFKA:
THE BUREAUCRAT AS ARTIST

Highlights of the Proceedings of the Kafka Conference held on June 3-4, 2024, the centennial of his death, at the CUNY Graduate Center, sponsored by The Center for the Humanities, Arts and Twenty-First Century Careers of the Hunter College School of Education, in conjunction with the Jewish Theological Seminary and FEGS (Federation Employment and Guidance Service), with funding provided, in part, by the Federation of Jewish Philanthropies and the Samuel J. and Ethel Lefrak Foundation.

31. The Wounded Body: Myth and Reality in Kafka's Work
Ari Politzer, Ph.D.*

Kafka had only to report to work each morning to enter the world of myth. The Workmen's Accident Insurance Institute for the Kingdom of Bohemia—an organization whose very name bespeaks the grotesque anatomy of the Austro-Hungarian Empire, a modern welfare state mounted on an aging monarchy—sought to counteract the spread of socialism among the working classes by constructing a secular ritual to replace the ancient law of *wergild* ("man-price"): bodies (or parts of bodies) of workers killed (or maimed) by the most up-to-date industrial technology in the world were to be ransomed by compensatory blood-money collected from the employers and distributed by an agency of the state.

Until the publication of *The Wounded Body*, in which I trace the influence of Kafka's work as a civil servant on Kafka's work as a writer, no one recognized the fault line running through the enlightened social welfare policies that it was Kafka's job to implement. For the purpose of lowering insurance costs by maximizing occupational safety, injuries were viewed as the inevitable by-product of design flaws in machines whose blades mutilated workers at a rate that could be predicted with a fair amount of precision. But for the purpose of insuring the workers and calculating fair rates for the premiums the business owners were to pay, the injuries were viewed as accidents. Now an accident whose occurrence

* Ari Politzer, Ph.D., is Professor of Anthropology, the Hebrew University of Jerusalem. His latest book is *More Than Real: On the History of the Moral Imagination in Czechoslovakia*.

can be forecast with a high degree of actuarial probability has been rationalized but at the same time returned to the realm of myth, where accidents reveal the hidden order of things. Here we encounter the dream logic of Kafka's world in which complicated arguments are staged: now one side, now another comes into view, but rather than coming into contact in open antithesis and possible resolution, they each nullify the other, to produce an impasse in which thinking becomes torturous.

In myth and in vestiges of the archaic world that survive in fewer and fewer forests and imaginations, evil and misfortune are not dissociated: punishment falls on man in the guise of misfortune, transforming all sufferings, all injuries, all disease, all failure into a sign of defilement.[1] This, too, evokes the dream logic of Kafka's stories. Kafka was obsessed with the wounded body, and made it the central image of "A Country Doctor," one of the few stories that satisfied him. Here, he tells of a phantasmagorical night journey that orbits around a wound that the doctor misses the first time he examines his patient, but then—"ah, now both horses were whinnying together [as they gazed at me through the window]; the noise, I supposed, was ordained by heaven to assist my [second] examination of the patient—and this time I discovered that the boy was indeed ill. On his right side, near the hip, was an open wound as big as the palm of my hand. Rose-red, in many variations, dark in the hollows, lighter at the edges, softly granulated, with regular clots of blood, open as a surface mine in the daylight. That was how it looked from a distance. But on a closer inspection there was another complication. I could not help a low whistle of surprise. Worms as thick and as long as my little finger, themselves rose-red and blood-spotted as well, were wriggling from their fastness in the interior of the wound towards the light, with small white heads and many little legs."[2] As fantasy, this image rises up out of Kafka's horror of the living Medusa: the vagina, or, more particularly, the vagina of women of his own class, which turned him to stone. Once he has discovered the "vagina-like wound," the doctor's clothes are stripped off his body by the boy's family and village elders.[3] They lay him down naked beside the boy, and the two are left alone to enact a kind of wedding rite that Kafka explicitly associates with the ancient beliefs and shamanic practices that are dying out in the doctor's district. Here fantasy is raised to the level of myth, and myth and reality seamlessly fit together in the image of a multilayered wound which resembles an excavation site that is harmful to workers (an open-pit mine) and that carries a trace of the most common injuries that Kafka encountered through his meticulous and persevering investigations as an insurance official: the severed hands and fingers of workers disabled on the job. This fecund image refracts the flight of the mind as it races away from the thing it can't bear to see and back toward the thing that holds it spellbound, fragmented by its attraction to and revulsion from one and the same thing: the wound in its hallucinatory, ritually and medically unclean, shape-changing aspect as the coal mine/dirty black hole/menstrual vagina/grave/coitus in which the penis falls off and spermatozoa morph into bacilli: the worms turn into "my little finger" which in turn suggests the diminutive male organ dismembered, defiled and sickened unto death by coitus, a sign of the venereal disease that plagued the minds and bodies of respectable men who in Kafka's day were accustomed to visiting brothels and, if they were men such as Kafka, closeting their homoerotic yearning.

Both Kafka's private suffering and the customary life of his time and place are lodged in that rose-red wound. It is the site of a threefold betrayal. At the start of the doctor's journey, as the magical horses carry him off into the night, he becomes blind and deaf to his betrayal of his servant-girl Rose; her name emphatically links her to the boy's "great wound." The doctor abandons Rose to his groom, although a moment earlier he sees the groom biting her neck and the girl fleeing into his house and locking the door, then he hears her shrieking as the groom splits and bursts the door and charges in to rape her. An instant later the doctor arrives at the house of his patient, and is forced to play a false role in an ancient healing rite. He lays with the boy "on the side of the wound," then, as a sign that he is already taking flight, the boy becomes merely a disembodied voice in his ear, a voice pouring out its despair. The doctor responds coldly, with a lie calculated to lull the enraged, mistrustful, pathetic boy into a false sense of security, and allow the doctor to make a safe getaway. 'Do you know,' said a voice in my ear, 'I have very little confidence in you. Why, you were only blown in here, you didn't come on your own feet. Instead of helping me, you're cramping me on my deathbed. What I'd like best is to scratch your eyes out.' 'Right,' I said, 'it is a shame. And yet I am a doctor. What am I to do? Believe me, it's not too easy for me either.' 'Am I supposed to be content with this apology? Oh, I must be, I can't help it. I always have to put up with things. A fine wound is all I brought into the world; that was my sole endowment.' 'My young friend,' said I, 'your mistake is: you have not a wide enough view. I have been in all the sickrooms, far and wide, and I can tell you: your wound is not so bad. Done in a tight spot with two strokes of the ax. Many a one proffers his side and can hardly hear the ax in the forest, far less that it is coming nearer to him.' 'Is that really so, or are you deluding me in my fever?' 'It is really so, take the word of honor of an official doctor.' And he took it and lay still. But now it was time for me to think of escaping."[4] The story ends with the doctor abandoning the dying boy and wandering endlessly over snowy roads, accursed in his belief that he is the victim of an evil fate. "Betrayed! Betrayed! A false alarm on the night bell once answered—it cannot be made good, not ever."[5] It is the fate of a man whose dissociated lust comes to haunt him in the image of an ax that appears inexplicably out of thin air and cuts a fatal wound in its victim's flesh. In that wound, the myth of the death-dealing female genitalia copulates with the everyday reality of workers' fingers sliced off by automated machines for cutting and shaping wood. The final betrayal appears only through what is left out of the image: the unseen hand that hurls the ax from a great distance, the distance that separates the doctor's acts from his awareness. The doctor has betrayed himself—and, as a result, the servant-girl and the boy who depend on him—by cutting himself off from the source of true and faithful relations to the world—his desire.

Kafka's stories are encoded autobiographical inquisitions; any outward resemblance between the characters and their author has been purged; what speaks through the characters are Kafka's personally-lived states of impossibility, the predicaments in love and work that he could never resolve. Kafka provides a reading model for his stories in his description of the rose-red wound and the doctor's examination of it: the meaning that lies on the surface belongs to everyday life and may be found in a cursory inspection, but the truest and most disturbing meanings come up from hidden depths and reveal the horror and hopelessness of the situation. In the bad faith of the doctor, I hear a trace of the writer's bad faith regarding his job as an insurance official who investigates the injuries of workers: "take the word of honor of an official doctor."[6] Herr Doktor Kafka, the title he earned with his law degree, was nothing if not divided. He hated the Institute, but when he took the side of respectable society, which he was perfectly capable of doing in the clear light of day, he saw the necessity of work that grounded him in real life and that gave cover to the all-too-vulnerable, indeed sick, artist, Franz Kafka, whose disembodied voice can also be heard in the story. This is the voice of the diaries and the letters to Felice, a voice *in extremis* that paradoxically sought justification in self-mortifying, self-evaluative ruminations that are refracted in the claim that "a fine wound is all I brought into the world."[7] The story of this wound, so remote in its surface details from Kafka's day-to-day life, could not have been written without his immersion in the field of accident insurance and the fire that it inflamed in him—the generative conflict between the conventional man and the artist.

Notes

1. See Paul Ricoeur, *The Symbolism of Evil*, translated by Emerson Buchanan (Boston: Beacon Press, 1967), 27.
2. Franz Kafka, "A Country Doctor," *Selected Short Stories of Franz Kafka*, translated by Willa and Edwin Muir (New York: The Modern Library, 1952), 153. Hereafter "Doctor."
3. Saul Friedländer, *Franz Kafka: The Poet of Shame and Guilt* (New Haven: Yale University Press, 2013), 102.
4. "Doctor," 154-155.
5. "Doctor," 156.
6. "Doctor," 155.
7. Ibid.

32. THE INVESTIGATOR MAKES HIS REPORT: ON KAFKA'S PROSE

Harry Mann, Ph.D.*

Kafka circulated copies of the Institute's annual reports among his literary friends, starring the sections that he had written. In 1908 and 1909, his first two years at the Institute, the young lawyer's contributions dealt mainly with legal issues, such as mandatory coverage in the construction industry, but he was also given writing assignments that lay outside his area of professional competence. His supervisor, Chief Inspector Eugen Pfohl, quickly discovered that his trainee combined a sharp eye for detail, a capacity for assimilating a vast body of technical knowledge with remarkable speed, a pedantic thoroughness, and investigative zeal, with a dedication to service and an unwavering smile for everyone on staff, from the Managing Director of the Institute to the messengers and typists and the woman who cleaned his office. He was liked by everyone; he alone never got into squabbles about Czech vs. German nationalism or office politics; he was, in sum, the ideal career bureaucrat, a quick study, a devoted civil servant, an accommodating man who welcomed rather than tried to wriggle out of the hard work his supervisors required of him. Kafka at the office, the other Kafka who impressed his superiors and rubbed shoulders with his contemporaries, still remains largely unknown; he continues to astonish everyone who knows only the legend of the anguished artist. But we

* Harry Mann, Ph.D., is Percy Uris Professor of Labor History, New York University. He is writing a book called *Kafka's Investigations* on hitherto unexamined relationships between Kafka's field work in factories and construction sites and the stories in which he deconstructed the machinery of social organization in modern times.

who have resurrected the other Kafka from archives in Prague, Berlin and Jerusalem would like you to share Eugen Pfohl's astonishment as he realized that there was no task that he could give his new supervisee that would exceed his talent. And so, at the start of his career, when Kafka was still an entry-level worker, he was asked to write on the then-novel question of motor vehicle operations at construction sites.

Kafka, it must be said, was one of two token Jews at the Institute. One of our conference directors, Rabbi Bryk, has suggested to me in a personal communication that Kafka's exceptional work at the office should not be understood merely as a natural outcome of his superior abilities, but as a result of his unique situation. It was a storm of excellence, Rabbi Bryk believes, produced by combining his gifts as a man and a writer with his insecurity as a Jew, who felt under continual pressure to try harder and be outstanding in order to maintain his standing in the exclusionary world where strings had to be pulled to get him admitted. I find this speculation quite plausible, but its persuasiveness too much depends on stereotypes drawn from the history of tokenism with which the emancipation of Jews in Europe was simultaneously implemented and stymied. At the time that he began working at the Institute, Kafka had sloughed off his Jewish identity; his sensitivity to anti-Semitism was a later development. I cannot rule out Rabbi Bryk's contention, but we have no direct evidence to support it. Quite the contrary: Kafka was treated with immense respect and consideration by Managing Director Robert Marschner and Chief Inspector Pfohl.

Kafka joined the staff of the Institute just at the moment when accident insurance came into its own as a powerful arm of the welfare state, a field of practice with an important contribution to make to the social good. The increased frequency and severity of industrial accidents were widely recognized as a technological problem that could not be eliminated and a social cause that could not make progress without a mobilization across disciplinary lines. Effective measures required the collaboration of Samaritans, technicians, and bureaucrats. Leaders in the emergent field organized international conferences that brought together everyone with even a remote interest in accidents: mountain guides, orderlies, railroaders, men of conscience, along with doctors, policy makers, engineers, and, of course, Kafka's superiors at the Institute, who invited Kafka to attend, so that he might experience the heady atmosphere of accident prophylaxis, which would foster his professional development. Motivated in part by his commitment to the cause, and in part by his desire to gain mastery over every aspect of occupational safety about which he was called upon to write, Kafka subscribed to journals on open-pit mines for quarrying various types of stone and on the various branches of the woodworking industry, two of the areas in which he became a specialist. He also audited engineering courses at night on his own time, and acquired a technical competence that few practitioners in the insurance industry could match. After less than two years on the job, he had already gained sufficient expertise to write an essay on "Accident Prevention Rules for Wood Planing Machines." Addressed to the owners of 32,000 businesses spread out over northern Bohemia, a catchment area too big for the Institute's seven traveling inspectors and its office staff of 250 specialists who had to investigate and process all the owners' compliance and payroll records and the injured workers' disability claims, Kafka used persuasion where effective regulation was impossible. It was a cunning piece of propaganda, a hidden polemic disguised as a totally objective discourse, a proving ground for the double-voiced prose whose positively technological and bureaucratic attention to detail would later heighten the weirdness and horror of his fiction. In his report on wood planing machines, he broke down the mechanisms that linked the manufacture of dominoes and toy weapons for children with the cost of insuring the workers, and depicted these oblique relationships in terms that his target audience would readily understand and accept. He promoted the use of a new, safe, cylindrical spindle as an improvement that would benefit the business owners in the long run by cutting the costs of the premiums they paid. This essay, included in the annual report for 1909, was the first of many triumphs that Kafka won for the Institute.

With his characteristic precision and modesty, Kafka pointed out to his friends that his contributions were actually the product of technical innovations and administrative laws introduced by anonymous researchers and men in high office over a period of twenty years, ever since the inception of social insurance as an ideological position and a state apparatus for mediating the legitimate claims of labor against capital. All that he had done, he insisted, was to assemble the material he had been given and present it "in straightforward and simple German prose."[1] The little asterisks set alongside selected passages told another story, and asserted his pride in a job well done.

With his literary friends, Kafka was alternately taciturn and witty, sincere and ironical, sometimes both in the same breath. We have no record of how they reacted when he showed them the Institute report, with his self-effacing words blown up, so to speak, by little star-bursts floating beside the pieces he authored. His friends must have realized at once that he was extending to his bureaucratic texts the same doubleness that marked his relation to the stories he read aloud to them: he was extravagantly self-deprecating beforehand, but when he came across something he found funny, he found it wildly funny, and his contagious laughter was shot-through with pride. And wasn't it significant that he called the texts in question "German prose" and described them as "straightforward and simple"? His friends must have found it hard to believe that he wasn't shadowboxing with language, as usual, evoking by reversal the words they associated with his prose, words such as "enigmatic," "multilayered," "resonant," words that led you far from the manifest content of his remark and highlighted the contrast between the writing he did by day and the writing he did by night.

The differences between the two must never be disregarded. He reserved the word "work" only for his artistic production; he called it his "lyric work."[2] A rigid distinction that abstracted it from his actual writing practice. Yet the man that suffers is never in the best position to understand the mind that creates; he can never retrace the obscure process through which mundane facts are turned into poetry. Nor can we. Nevertheless, we can show the links between the two kinds of writing. If you substitute "images acutely visualized" and "lucid" for "straightforward," and "sounds effortless" or better yet "sounds spontaneous" for "simple," you will find the terms that equate his Institute-related writing and his poetic work, in which hallucinatory images and phrasing saturated with intense emotion disturb the normal prose syntax of stories that take the form of investigations and reports.

But how likely is it that his friends thought of this?

Their very solidarity with the suffering man, who complained bitterly about the time he lost in the office, disqualified them from seeing that the writer of the bureaucratic and the poetic prose was the same genre-dissolving author. Moreover, they lacked the perspective that we have attained through a century of Kafka research. They couldn't have known, for example, that in speaking of his administrative and legal writing as "straightforward and simple," he was paraphrasing the laudatory, in fact gushing evaluation of his job performance that Pfohl wrote at the end of his first year. Kafka, who in a letter to his boss told him he loved him like a son, couldn't take in and derive any increment of self- and job-satisfaction which an employee with less lofty aims and a less perfectionistic sensibility would have obtained from his mentor's high regard.

Kafka's unusual combination of technological, insurance-specific and legal knowledge, his unique capacity for synthesizing their interrelation in razor-sharp arguments supported by statistical data organized in tables whose message was evident at a glance—this made him indispensable to Pfohl and Marschner. Overburdened themselves, they could confidently hand over to him the files that were piling up on their desks. They gave him the most difficult cases: correspondence with business owners who were protesting the new premiums set by the Institute after its staff uncovered fraud in their payroll accounts; internal audits; articles for newspapers on the Institute's social mission; speeches that the Managing Director and the Chief Inspector presented at major conferences. Not only did Kafka unfailingly turn in everything they asked of him on time, his work almost never needed any revision. He seemed to divine just what his superiors would have said if they had been granted the time to write it themselves.

Never before had they had the occasion to call an Institute text produced in the line of duty a tour de force. In recognition of his extraordinary talent, he rose rapidly through the ranks. In October 1909, after hardly more than a year of service, he was officially made a trainee; in May 1910, he earned the title of draftsman; in February 1911, he was appointed executive, and a short time later, deputy department head. Pfohl stated that "without Kafka, the whole department would collapse."[3] At the time of his retirement in 1922, Kafka was senior secretary of the Institute.

Through the long slow exhumation and multidisciplinary study of the corpus of Kafka's writings, we have gradually come to understand the significance of his daily work at the Institute, and, more specifically, the interdependence between his work as a bureaucrat and his work as an artist. Kafka, as the go-to deputy head of his department, was sent on tours of the industrial towns of Bohemia to hold what we would nowadays call town meetings as well as handle delicate negotiations with groups of irate business owners. These tours equipped him with first-hand knowledge of how the factories operated, which strengthened his hand in his dealings with the owners, and also afforded him intimate glimpses of life and work that fed his imagination to the advantage of his art. His studies of unsafe machinery and working conditions were to save the lives and limbs of hundreds of workers in the lumber mills and factories of Bohemia, but they were also to enter into his authoritative account of the writing machine that executes the death sentence in the penal colony and of a flat star-shaped spool named Odradek, the spool for broken-off bits of thread that is animated with a life of its own, like a moving part that escaped from the burgeoning garment industry in which factory owners were investing their capital or a fetish into which garment workers were pouring their living labor. The verbal surface of Kafka's art can be described as a fusion of technological language and metonymic figures of speech whose meaning slides away from the thing he's just said; this kind of linguistic wizardry made him a dangerous adversary of the business owners. In his encounters with them, he would sound impartial even as he sounded like one of them; he would put forward their arguments better than they and at the same time drain them of sense and cogency. In the end, it seemed that they themselves, rather than he, expected them to improve their business practices. If they did manage to resist, he brought them to court and successfully litigated the Institute's case against them. He went home without any feeling of triumph, until he reproduced something of the subject matter and matter-of-fact style of his investigative reports and legal briefs in his fiction.

Notes

For information regarding Kafka's bureaucratic career, the author is indebted to Ernst Pawel's *The Nightmare of Reason: A Life of Franz Kafka* (New York: The Noonday Press, 1984) pp. 183-190, and to Reiner Stach's *Kafka: The Decisive Years*, translated by Shelley Frisch (Princeton: Princeton University Press, 2013) pp. 26-27, 284-291, 364-365. Hereafter *Nightmare of Reason* and *Decisive Years*.

1. This phrase epitomizes the quality of Kafka's writing that was valued and praised by his superiors in their job evaluations of him throughout his career. See *Nightmare of Reason*, 186.
2. *Decisive Years*, 291.
3. *Nightmare of Reason*, 188.

33. Change of Program:
Announcements and Apologies
Bernard Hoch, Ed.D.*

Before we break for lunch, I have a couple of announcements to make. The Mayor has issued a weather advisory; they want everyone off the streets except first responders and auxiliary personnel. Conditions out there have got a lot worse over the past two hours, but there's no reason for anyone to leave the building. We've catered a hot kosher lunch for you in the lobby.

I also have some disappointing news. We have received word that Dr. Bergson won't be able to deliver his keynote address after all. As I announced this morning when we rescheduled his paper from the beginning to the end of the day, Hurricane Trisha forced his flight from Houston to be rerouted to Cleveland Airport; now it appears that Hurricane Ursula has shut down CLE Airport. Dr. Bergson has emailed his paper to Dr. Gornisht-Helfn, a close colleague of his, who agreed to read it in his stead.

This, however, has necessitated another change in the program. Dr. Ken Gornisht-Helfn has been called upon to provide psychiatric back-up at the Bellevue ER. He won't be able to get here until his shift ends at 6:30 p.m. It is most distressing to Rabbi Bryk and myself that we will have to run later than expected, but I guarantee that you will find Dr.

* Bernard Hoch, Ed.D., is Deputy Director, The Center for the Humanities, Arts and Twenty-First Century Careers of the Hunter College School of Education. His articles on the creative arts and technology in professional education appear regularly in the *Journal of Education and Practice*. His essay on Kafka, "The Writer in His Two Professions," was recently published in *Thresholds Review*. With Rabbi Bryk, he is co-director of the Kafka Conference.

Bergson's contribution well worth waiting for. Please accept our apologies. We've done everything we can to accommodate you in this time of emergency.

Holding the conference at all was a difficult call, with the subways out and the storm battering the city. We commend those of you who braved the severe weather to be with us today. Again, our apologies, and thanks to all of you for your interest in our project.

[*Scattered applause.*]

34. Excerpts from Dr. Bergson's Paper: The Hypnoidal Storyteller

Introductory Remarks by Ken Gornisht-Helfn, M.D.*

Vice-Chancellor Greenberg, Professor Hoch, Rabbi Bryk, honored presenters and members of the audience: In inviting Dr. Bergson to give the keynote address, the co-directors of the Conference asked him to help us unveil the truth about the living Kafka, to help us understand why he chose to spend his adult life shuttling every day back and forth, fiercely dedicated to his dual careers as artist and bureaucrat. The paper opens by posing but reframing this question, and closes by formulating—through the concepts of "dissociative process" and "hypnoidal images"—a way of understanding the resonant depth of Kafka's storytelling and the complex truth of the interrelation between the working artist and the civil servant who was a pioneer of occupational safety. In part two of the paper, Dr. Bergson explores the core question through a detailed analysis of *The Metamorphosis*. Here, he lays out and exemplifies the theory of dissociative process, links it to his practice as a working analyst and reaches his conclusion: the two careers are neither totally antithetical nor totally interdependent; they are mutually formative. Today, given the lateness of the hour and the length of the paper, I will present only parts one and three of Dr. Bergson's lecture; however, these sections can stand alone; and so can

* Daniel Bergson, M.D., is Training and Supervising Analyst, The American Institute for Psychoanalysis; Clinical Professor of Psychiatry, SUNY Downstate Medical Center; and Visiting Professor of Medical Humanities, The Thomas R. Cole Center for Health, Humanities and the Human Spirit of The University of Texas Medical School at Houston. With Ken Gornisht-Helfn, M.D., he co-edited *Dissociative Phenomena, Object Relations and the Self.*

part two, which deepens the interpretation of the narrative images that are discussed throughout the paper. In the end, we will be able to make the whole of this illuminating work available to the public by publishing part two separately, as the Appendix of the volume of conference papers that Rabbi Bryk is editing. And now, "The Hypnoidal Storyteller" by Daniel Bergson:

I know how serious you are about confronting the truth of Kafka's difficulties in living and working. But for Kafka, truth lies in an abyss—abyss is one of his key words—that can't be confronted. There is no shortcut to it. You have to wander "along senseless paths" to come close to it.[1] Along the way you have to lose everything you thought you knew. Hope has a logic of its own, and this is the logic we cling to, confusing it with logic as such, the logic that adheres to things as they are and remains indifferent to us. At the end of *The Trial*, just before K. is executed, Kafka writes, "Logic is doubtless unshakable, but it cannot withstand a man who wants to go on living."[2] K. knows and doesn't know what is about to happen. Kafka's abyss is situated in this dissociative state, but he labors hard to bring it into the realm of the visible so that we may catch a glimpse of it.

Two gentlemen in frock coats and top hats lead K. to a small stone quarry at the end of the town, just beside an urban apartment house. One of the officials investigates the quarry to find a suitable spot where they expect the guilt-ridden man to take the long, thin, double-edged butcher knife they offer him and plunge it through his breast. The right spot is found "near the cliffside where a loose boulder was lying."[3] K. willingly allows himself to be brought there, laid down on the ground with his head settled on the boulder, like Jacob in the "dreadful place" where he dreams of a ladder between the earth and heaven;[4] and in that position, K. surrenders to the abyss even as he resists it. He has a reverie that raises the writing to the level of prayer; it is a revelation, among other things of the dreamlike state in which images came unbidden to Kafka: "His glance fell on the top story of the house adjoining the quarry. With a flicker as of a light going up, the casements of a window there suddenly flew open; a human figure, faint and insubstantial at that distance and at that height, leaned abruptly forward and stretched both arms still farther. Who was it? A friend? A good man? Someone who sympathized? Someone who wanted to help? Was it one person only? Or was it mankind? Was help at hand?"[5] That gesture—those outstretched arms—beckoned to the latent religiosity of Kafka's newly enlightened bourgeois German-speaking contemporaries such as Brod, and misled them into reading Kafka as a religious allegorist. This passage trembles at the brink of expressing the universal desire of humankind to be saved, but the reach of its feeling, its nearly infinite sorrow, comes from under-cutting K.'s desperate yearning with dramatic irony. The story answers the question of whether help was at hand in the negative.

Only by following Kafka to his abyss—an abyss he reaches by way of his two professions—can we fathom the full measure of his achievement. Diagnostic terms such as "rapid cycling in and out of psychotic depression" or "severely schizoid" might be helpful as a stay against helplessness if I were treating Kafka as my patient, but even then I would have to jettison them and let myself be taken by his train of thought into his strange frozen state. Here, the old terms of authority, by which the doctor secures his position as an official doctor and loses the patient, are no less out of place: they blunt—more than that, they betray—the experience that has been entrusted to me to get across to you, the experience that Kafka struggled to keep hidden from the people closest to him, who, by their very closeness, presented the greatest danger to him. What he endured in isolation was terrifying. His primary relation to other people was fear and indifference. His primary relation to himself was hatred of his weakness. He needed to keep his guilt and self-loathing hidden, and he felt a tremendous need to make his inner world known. With rare exceptions, he could only do so obliquely and in writing.

In my chapter on Kafka in *The Quiet Horror of Everyday Life: Psychic Deadness and Transformation*, I describe an elderly German-Jewish woman, a Holocaust survivor with whom I worked during the last twelve years of her life. Before coming to me, Alice R. had spent nearly fifty years in treatment, going from one therapist to another. None of them could bear sitting with the experiences she brought them; each in turn felt excluded by her immersion in trance-like states and reduced to helplessness by what she demanded of them: they had to sit still, session after session, for months, years, eternities, and listen, do nothing but listen to the stories she told them. She spent whole sessions engaged in what I came to think of as hypnoidal storytelling. Bizarre images floated up into consciousness, she watched their metamorphosis into characters of a story that she would narrate in a hushed, matter-of-fact voice, spellbound as if she were watching a film. Two trees with their branches lopped away and their bark stripped off, two bare trunks driven into the sand, set up side-by-side on a deserted beach, look out at the sea—these were the protagonists of a story to which she kept returning. Eventually a lifeguard stand appears, then a lifeguard, who watches her as a girl splashing around near the shoreline, then wading into the water, and then swimming. This progression took many years of going nowhere together.

At one point she warned me that no matter what I saw or how I felt, I must keep my seat, and under no circumstances dive into her story and try to save her.

The most horrific story she told me begins with her as a chicken trussed on her mother's cutting board, about to be salted, put in the oven, roasted and carved into thin slices. Hearing this, I remembered something that Kafka confessed to Brod during the crisis of October, 1912, when he was panicked by Felice's acceptance of his marriage proposal. "Dearest Max!" he wrote, "[G]iven the way I am, I would be best off keeping out of sight. That would be the correct course. At least I used to be able to cling to the office if there was no other way. These days, however, the best I could do would be to throw myself at my director's feet and beg him not to throw me out, appealing to his compassion (I don't see any other reason, even though everyone sees things quite differently, which is lucky), if I were to follow nothing but my wishes, and I have very few inhibitions. Every day fantasies fill my head, for example, that I lie stretched out on the ground, sliced up like a roast, and with my hand I am slowly pushing a piece of its meat to a dog in the corner. Yesterday I sent my great confession to [Felice in] Berlin."[6]

In an instant, through the near-identity of Kafka's and my patient's ghastly self-images, I grasped the process—the dissociative process—that supplied Kafka with metaphors for poetry, metaphors with the uncanny power to hold readers in thrall, to induce in us the trance-like state in which their author first received them. As if this weren't already enough, I saw in a flash, on the basis of my intimacy with Alice R., the dissociation was not only the medium of Kafka's revelations, but that, in his most perfectly realized story, *The Metamorphosis*, it is part of "the message," the part we hear without hearing and see without seeing; it is precisely this aspect of the story that produces its hypnotic effect.

Here I imagine somebody is thinking that she has caught me in a contradiction, that if protocol permitted her to stand up and speak, she would raise the following objection: Earlier, you threw aside clinical language so that you and we might approach Kafka's experience without a veil of formulation blurring our reception of it. But then you privilege the idea of dissociation, and argue that it is the key to unlocking Kafka's mystery. And I would have to answer: You are right. But I am, after all, a clinical worker. I can't carry on my practice without becoming caught up in contradictions. Nor can I carry it on without clinical terms. I try to shed what I have known and thought in order to hover in the space of scientific unknowing, what keeps me afloat is my desire to come into contact with the clinical data. It is the hardest thing in the world to find the data, they slither from one disguise to another, and they're quickly lost in the fog of ideas, which I can't help trying out as I pursue a vague sensation or feeling that startles me. I draw nearer to it when I have nothing in mind but being with whatever it is that startled me, but then want to grasp it in an interpretation, to form a concept of it, and again it eludes me. Finally, I just watch it unfold until it hits me: dissociation is the concept that grants access to the depth and elusiveness that mark the data of Kafka's writing. It feels as if the data were thinking, not I. As if on its own, the unformulated experience takes form, and I see it. In writing Kafka mines his shifting self-states, he discovers the peculiar sense of depth that arises from the ghostly presence alongside an emotional state of a contrary or incompatible state, he raises the dissociated elements into consciousness and mixes them together, despair in hope or happiness in sorrow, or rage in tenderness, or inhumanity in humanity, or he traces the slithering away of one thing into another or into no-thing.

Kafka lived "in great perplexity,"[7] perpetually indecisive, taking a position, intensifying and reversing it a moment later, wavering between one side and the other, weaving the counterposed strands of his stories on the loom of his dissociative way of being. Gregor Samsa's empathy for his sister reaches its pinnacle a moment before she takes charge of the family's desperate situation and tells her parents that they must no longer think of the filthy invader into their living room as a "he" but as an "it," and they "have to try to get rid of it."[8] She, who has fed him and cared for him when his parents and the Managing Director have backed away from him in horror, becomes his most brutal enemy. The entire story is built up of such oppositions within and between characters.

Of these, none is more shocking, more comic and terrible, than the contrast between Gregor's human feelings and expectations and the inhumanity of the people he most loves and values. But this is motivated and rendered inevitable by the split built into the image that sets the narrative going: the contrast between Gregor's outward appearance as a gigantic insect and the human proclivities he retains until his last breath. The barbarous treatment he receives is "naturalized" by the stranger he becomes, yet, the story suggests, his transformation is a conversion into bodily form of the thing that Gregor cannot think or say, namely, his shame and protest against his ill-treatment all along by his family and the firm that employs him. Kafka sets the logic of cause-and-effect spinning, only to arrest our attention in the area of ultimate concern he creates, the area in which Gregor's gigantic human deficits are lucidly itemized as if before a tribunal that adds them to the charges leveled against Gregor's world.

Kafka was in equal measure a conformist, or rather a hyperconformist, and a critic of culture, a critic so radical that he abandoned hope for his civilization. When it came to organizing his life, that is to say, his writing life, since he only felt truly alive when writing, he did so bureaucratically, in conformity with Weber's "iron cage of life," the dominant social structure of his time and place. Weber divided the human life cycle into three boxes—education, work, and retirement—a division that the beneficence of the welfare state would make inevitable to the masses, who would willingly climb into their cages where they would be well-fed and cared for. The bureaucratized life cycle met the needs of the industrialized world for trained workers who would strive to adapt themselves to the rapidly changing uses that their society had for them. In this vein, Kafka, with Brod's encouragement, compartmentalized the documentary and imaginative writing he did, the former task assigned to him by his bosses, the latter self-assigned, according to strict schedules he continually had to revise, at the behest of his moods or circumstances beyond his control; he further separated his day labor and his night work by allocating them, and the capacities associated with them, distinct sites of production, the former confined as much as possible to his office, the latter to his room, in accordance with the principle of the division of labor that maximized the efficiency of bureaucratic departments and assembly lines. Brod advised him to increase the rationality and professionalism of his writing practice by working on only one story or novel at a time, rather than jump from one thing to another as the impulse took him, and also to write each work sequentially rather than drift among segments whose relation to each other and a unified plot was probably not apparent even to him, and so left him open to wasting his time on endless divagations.

No matter how hard he tried to do this, every effort to bring order to his writing life broke down. The two spheres of his writing wouldn't stay sealed off from each other, fortunately, for a certain degree of breakdown enhanced his production in each of his segregated domains of writing, contributing writerly craft to the documents he turned out at the office, and contributing details charged with experience of the work world to his stories. Nonetheless, the crossover between the two worlds benefited each of them only up to a point; then it paralyzed him. He could no longer contain his doubleness, he felt under siege by the world in his writing room. Gregor's sister and mother, in their effort to make Gregor more comfortable, come to remove the human furniture from his room, so that he can move freely about, crisscrossing an open space, literally climbing the walls and hanging upside down from the ceiling. There, he rocks back and forth in a way that suggests the davening of the divided figure idealized by the Jewish Enlightenment—the man in the street who remains a Jew at home. It also suggests the masturbation of the poor traveler—Gregor is "a traveling salesman" who lives out of a suitcase, far from home, lonely and socially isolated.[9] Gregor's momentary feeling that he is being well cared for collapses; he doubts that he wants his room emptied "at the price of simultaneously swiftly and completely forgetting his human past."[10] He thrusts his head out of the sheet under which he has covered it, and rushes out in a futile attempt to rescue his writing desk; he charges, changes direction four times, and ends up soothing his hot belly against the glass of a framed picture of a woman in furs which he had recently cut out of a magazine, an image reminiscent of Sachor-Masoch's *Venus in Fur*. He is unable to save the chest of drawers that held his fret saw and the other tools he loved working with. Or can he retain the desk at which he had written his homework assignments as a student at the commercial academy, and as a secondary and even primary school pupil."[11] This desk is the material storehouse of all his memories of the education that transformed the boy-child into a working man as well as the home office where he does his paperwork at 4 a.m. before rushing out to catch his train; it is his own place of personal development and also the place of business from which he sets out every day with "particular zeal" to serve his chief and his firm with utmost devotion to duty. [12] All was well when it was the central object in his room and seamlessly fused the first and second boxes of "the iron cage of life," education and work; losing it threatens to destroy his residual sense of human identity.

Gregor's room, like Kafka's, is situated between the living room and his parents' bedroom, but it also adjoins his sister's bedroom; it is totally enclosed, yet it is as much an extension of the other rooms, a passageway onto which they open, as it is a place apart. Gregor's desk, as already noted, belongs as much to his office life as to his narrow personal life in his room. With its three French doors, which are vertically split in the middle, this room doesn't afford Gregor boundaries that he can defend against his family or his company. The walls that Kafka wanted to put in place between poetic and bureaucratic writing were literal and rational, but they could not stand, for three reasons that overran his efforts to rationalize his writerly production. The first had to do with something he considered a weakness in himself, his dependence upon inspiration. The second is inseparable from the first, it restates the first in terms of an ordinary psychological process, dissociation. The third, which I will touch on later, has to do with Kafka's relation to language.

The bureaucratic order to which Kafka aspired, as a man of his time and place, was undermined by a process that came and went of its own accord—the dreamlike inner life out of which his stories began. In his reveries, he evoked the office life and the travels of the company man to the shop floors in the far north, evoked them in his own self and merged them with images that came out of the iron cage of his hunger art, filled him with energy and purpose and set him free to speak unspeakable things. Perhaps the most characteristic of these images carries the shock delivered by the matter-of-fact opening sentence of *The Metamorphosis*: "When Gregor Samsa woke one morning from troubled dreams, he found himself transformed right there in his bed into some sort of monstrous insect."[13] Gregor is floating in the hypnoidal state in which he first appeared to his author.

*

Earlier, I said that three factors undermined Kafka's efforts to organize his writing bureaucratically. The first two—inspiration and dissociation—are hardly the same, but in Kafka they were inseparably linked. Dissociation screened out the noisy world and allowed him to give himself over to internal images that came unbidden. Inspiration, for Kafka, was a special relationship to what arose in him then, a relationship of utmost attention, of receptivity, a spaciousness within that opened onto the heavens and contained revelations. At such moments, internal objects that ordinarily persecuted him were transformed, he surrendered to them and they held him in a relationship of prayer. The third factor also has to do with a special relationship, his relationship to language, the medium in which he carried out his search for purity, the craft by which he reached beyond his habitual fear and helplessness to "go over" the barriers that separated reality and parable.[14]

Professor Mann has laid out the institutional context for understanding the hopelessness of Kafka's attempt to separate his imaginative from his documentary writing. By detailing his job responsibilities, Professor Mann makes it abundantly clear that Kafka served the Institute primarily as a writer. And as a writer, he could be nothing less than himself, a master. But at the office, the master had to submit to another master, and his outward compliance belied his inner refusal to do so. His desire, a poet's desire to strip the language he uses of impurities, was absolute; but writerly craft, expended on official documents, was wasted, sullied. Rainer Stach has offered an insightful description and analysis of how the medium in which Kafka experienced emancipatory flight also bound and tortured him. In his chapter on "The Working World: High Tech and the Ghosts of Bureaucracy," Stach writes: "The days and nights of Kafka's life and labor too closely resembled each other...[A]t his desk late at night he was a 'first-rate draftsman,' and at the office he couldn't bear to settle for any wording that was second best. He never left the medium in which he could breathe: language. He longed for clarity and precision in every situation; the texts he wrote on behalf of the Institute are ample proof of this. His style comes through even when standard bureaucratic turns of phrase are used.... What tormented him was the endeavor to come up with the most precise linguistic expression for trivial matters."[15]

Here, based on his close reading of the textual evidence, Stach retrieves for the realm of fact the quixotic quest that Kafka engaged in at the office: he wanted to transmute impersonal communiqués into stylized communications that would bear the imprint of his singularity, his artistry. And Stach accounts for the added and finally impossible burden that Kafka took upon himself as rooted in the poet's relationship to language, his surplus concern with finding just the right words, which waver between exact denotation and conveying something that can only be suggested by their cadences, their sounds. Stach's insight is unimpeachable and decisive, but it is also opaque and open-ended. He has no need to inquire further into what drove Kafka to treat official documents as if they were literary texts, but I do. I understand this need to keep his nighttime practice alive during the day as repetition compulsion, the effort to reenact a trauma in the hope of mastering it. The private task he set himself at the office, that of turning the assignments his supervisors gave him into his own work, lyrical work, was the act of resistance by which he carved out a hidden sphere of independence from those supervisors, while appearing all the more zealous in carrying out their orders. This returned him to the position of covert rebellion in which he struggled at home, and it led inevitably back to the site of self-dismemberment: to fantasies of taking a knife to his body and carving himself up like a roast. Stach quotes the following passage from the *Diaries* to show the toll that Kafka's self-tormenting discipline took on him: "Finally I have the word 'stigmatize' and the appropriate sentence, but I am still holding all of it in my mouth with revulsion and a feeling of shame, as though it were raw flesh cut out of me (that is how much effort it cost me). Finally I say it, but keep hold of the great fear that everything in me is ready for lyrical work, and a work of that kind would be a heavenly resolution and a real coming alive for me, while here, in the office, because of such a wretched document I have to tear from a body capable of such happiness a piece of my flesh."[16]

The *Diaries* are that part of the Kafka canon in which he most freely and directly encounters himself under the gaze of his genius for self-observation. Yet in the *Diaries* he merely repeats with growing intensity his hatred of the office; here, in a matter of supreme importance for his happiness and even his survival, he fails to do the one thing that marks his writing as an artist and a bureaucrat: he never investigates what forces are congealed in his injurious relationship to the office.

If Kafka's office job drove him to mad states, why did he pursue his career at the Institute so vigorously? Why was it impossible for him to leave the job until advancing tuberculosis left him no choice? It makes no sense—unless we remember his doubleness, an effect of the dissociative process that permeates his life and his work; it was the whirlwind he rode from one self-state to another. We must hold in mind the overarching perspective from which he evoked the depths in which contrary emotional states are co-present; he attained this sublime perspective in his art, but couldn't sustain it in living his life and chronicling it in his diaries and letters. In reading them, we must never forget that when a dissociative person is in self-state A, he is largely or totally denied access to self-state B, so that he is continually losing his way and wandering senselessly in what he continually rediscovers are ever-narrowing circles. For this reason, it would be a mistake to take his endlessly repeated complaints about the office at face value. Yes, in writing the diaries and letters, he experienced rage and misery at the waste of his time and talent; but for many, if not most of the fifteen years that he worked at the Institute, he only hated the office when he was away from it. Once there, he was absorbed in the work at hand.

Notes

1. Franz Kafka, "Reflections on Sin, Pain, Hope, and the True Way," *The Great Wall of China: Stories and Reflections*, translated by Willa and Edwin Muir (New York: Schocken Books, 1961), 93.
2. Franz Kafka, *The Trial*, translated by Willa and Edwin

Muir (New York: Vintage Books, 1970), 286. Hereafter *Trial*.

3. *Trial*, 285.

4. Genesis 28:17.

5. *Trial*, 285-286.

6. Shelley Frisch's translation of Kafka's "Letter to Max Brod," 4/3/1913, quoted by Reiner Stach in *The Decisive Years*, translated by Shelley Frisch (Princeton: Princeton University Press, 2013), 276. Hereafter *Decisive Years*. See Franz Kafka, "Letter to Max Brod," 4/3/1913, *Letters to Friends, Family, and Editors*, translated by Richard and Clara Winston (New York: Schocken Books, 1977), 95.

7. "I was in great perplexity" is the opening statement of "A Country Doctor." See Franz Kafka, "A Country Doctor," *The Penal Colony: Stories and Short Pieces*, translated by Willa and Edwin Muir (New York: Schocken Books, 1961), 136. Hereafter *Penal Colony*.

8. Franz Kafka, *The Metamorphosis*, translated by Susan Bernofsky (New York: W.W. Norton & Company, 2014), 105. Hereafter *Metamorphosis*.

9. *Metamorphosis*, 22.

10. *Metamorphosis*, 74.

11. *Metamorphosis*, 77.

12. *Metamorphosis*, 63.

13. *Metamorphosis*, 21.

14. Franz Kafka, "On Parables," *Parables and Paradoxes*, translated by Willa and Edwin Muir, and Others (New York: Schocken Books, 1946), 11.

15. *Decisive Years*, 290-291.

16. Shelley Frisch's translation of Kafka, *Diaries*, 10/3/1911, quoted by Stach in *Decisive Years*, 291. See Franz Kafka, *Diaries*, 10/3/1911, edited by Max Brod, translated by Joseph Kresh (New York: Schocken Books, 1948), 62.

35. Rare Talent and Devotion to Duty:
Kafka's Example
Vicky Alaimo, M.A.*

I want to begin by thanking Professor Hock and Rabbi Bryk for inviting me to participate in this marvelous conference. It's late in the day, you've sat through many thought-provoking presentations, so let me acknowledge straightaway that I'm not a Kafka scholar, which I hope will afford you some relief, since the task of unpacking even a brief Kafka text requires the scholars to go on at some length, and the best that they can manage, as far as I can tell, is to show how Kafka's writing eludes all efforts to explain it. No, I don't mean that as a little joke. I, too, feel the presence of a mystery when I read Kafka, but it's not my job to account for it. I'm an Arts Administrator. And I speak from that perspective.

Kafka went to great lengths to please his superiors. We must be grateful to Professor Mann for his book, *Kafka at the Office*, and for the detailed narrative he has given us today. The takeaway here is that Kafka's responsibilities multiplied as his supervisor, Eugen Pfohl, discovered that there was nothing that Kafka wasn't ready, willing and able to do. Professor Mann referred in passing to the glowing evaluation that Kafka received at the end of his first year at the Institute, but I think it's important that you hear the text that Pfohl actually wrote. Pfohl begins soberly, qualifying his assessment of Kafka's ability as a writer, but he almost immediately gives

* Vicky Alaimo, M.A., is Director, The Writing Project, National Council on the Arts. She is spearheading NCOA's oral history project, which will interview PEN authors to provide a national archive and database on the dual careers of working artists.

up the convention that requires strengths to be offset by limitations, especially in the case of new hires. Because of Kafka's talent for summing up complex subject matter in straightforward language, he fairly sings Kafka's praises. Listen to this: Dr. Kafka's work is marked by his "exceptional faculty for conceptualization. [He] combines outstanding zeal with sustained interest in all assignments."[1] Fifteen years later, his annual evaluation—he was by this time First Secretary of the Institute—had not withered into grudging acknowledgment of gifts with which everyone was by now familiar. The last line of the last evaluation, in recommending a substantial pay increase, states: "Dr. Kafka continues to serve the Institute as an eminently hardworking employee with rare talent and devotion to duty."[2]

The fact was that Dr. Kafka could no longer continue serving the Institute. Because of his advancing TB, he spent more time in sanatoria than he did at the office. This final evaluation was written either by a somewhat deluded but sympathetic man, blinded by his wish that his cherished associate remain well enough to carry on with his work, or by a clear-sighted and devoted, more than devoted, yes, deeply caring, administrator who didn't want his long-time colleague to go out with a black mark on his permanent record. In lieu of an evaluation that took note of his diminished capacities, he wrote the review that Kafka had earned through his rare talent and long years of devoted service.

All the archival materials that have recently been made available in *The Kafka Casebook*—inter-office memoranda, evaluations, oral history interviews with colleagues, and other documents—tell the same story. Franz Kafka took his work at the Institute seriously. Despite whatever ambivalence he may have felt, and there can be no question that he felt a certain ambivalence, he was convinced that it behooved him to do a first-rate job. His example, I submit, ought to be an inspiration to the many gifted writers and other artists who have entered our school systems and arts bureaucracies in such significant numbers ever since Arts-in-Education developed from a fledgling movement of poets to an established component of curricula for various subjects at all grade levels.

Notes

1. Ernst Pawel quotes Pfohl's evaluation in *The Nightmare of Reason: A Life of Franz Kafka* (New York: The Noonday Press, 1984), 186.
2. Ibid.

36. The Relationship of Prayer:
Concluding Remarks
Rabbi I. B. Bryk*

I have the happy task of thanking our presenters and offering a few concluding remarks.

Our presenters have once and for all demonstrated the fallacy of the old simple opposition between Kafka's office job and his literary work, an opposition that has lingered in the description and evaluation of his life and work long after this notion should have been put to rest. We have done that. I want to single out Professors Politzer and Mann for showing that Kafka's professional experience as an insurance official immeasurably enriched his fiction, providing him with material that was at the cutting edge of the modern world, and with metaphors that extended the reach of his storytelling into the realm of technology and social organization. Their description of the objective conditions refracted in Kafka's art set the stage, so to speak, for Dr. Bergson's taking us farther than we have gone before into the labyrinth of Kafka's internal world, and disclosing the law governing his productive life and what he made of it—the various quests for justification or recognition or belonging or safety or meaning or escape or disappearance that he invented for

* Rabbi I. B. Bryk is Director of Spiritual Care and the Diane and Arnold Jacobson Professor of Talmud and Rabbinics at the Jewish Theological Seminary. Known for the quality of his scholarship and his dynamic teaching, Rabbi Bryk is the author of more than forty books on modern Jewish theology, including *Between Man and Man: The Ethical Teaching of Buber, Rosenzweig, and Kafka*. His magnum opus, *The Fire, the Prayer, and the Place in the Woods: Problems in the Transmission of Tradition* includes a chapter on "Kafka's Hasidic Thought." With Professor Hoch, he is co-director of the Kafka Conference.

his protagonists. I know that many of you feel, as I do, that Dr. Bergson has made a substantial contribution to Kafka studies, and for this we can only be tremendously grateful. Using the latest psychological and neurological research, he has documented the degree to which dissociative phenomena pervaded Kafka's life and work, and shown beyond the shadow of a doubt that we can't take his complaints about the office at face value.

We each find our way into Kafka from our different perspectives, and if we come away confirmed in our beliefs and method of inquiry we have failed to encounter him. I approach him as a traditional Jew; he unsettles my relation to the Tradition, even as he invigorates it by my debate with him. Those of you raised in yeshivas, as I was, know that in Talmudic discussion an argument that threatens to resolve a controversy is called a difficulty (*kushia*) while one that keeps it open is called a solution (*teruz*). Listening to the presentations yesterday and today, I thought: each of us, from our different positions, seeks to resolve the debate in defense of our own position and keep it open in the areas in which we are free to follow the inquiry wherever it leads us. I was particularly struck by the conjunction of *kushia* and *teruz*— of a problematic effort of closure with an opening of new ground for the problematic—in Dr. Bergson's presentation on hypnoidal storytelling. Dr. Bergson tries to enclose the question of Kafka's religious thought in the clearly inadequate formulation of it as allegory. For him, as a secular humanist, the question holds little life and can be disposed of with a phrase. Yet where he is free to follow Kafka, into the Kafkan abyss, as he puts it, he extends the range of our capacity to think what we feel: the sublime in Kafka is constituted by the co-presence of incommensurable elements, which Kafka represents as echoes of spiritual struggle. Elsewhere, in his book on dissociative phenomena, Dr. Bergson takes up the question of the resonant depths in Kafka and offers a detailed analysis of the process by which he forms them. In his day-to-day life, Kafka suffered from a neurotic sensitivity to noise, which he transmuted through experiencing it as the assault of cacophonous profane life on the realm of his sacred writing. He turned his daily struggle into the arena for looking deeply into himself and raising up or spiritualizing what he found there. In the uncanny resonance of his sublime passages, religious readers, beginning with Brod and continuing down to our own day, hear Kafka's yearning for redemption amidst echoes of the Incommensurable. According to Dr. Bergson, such passages are produced by Kafka's transcending or at least lightening the barrier—the wall of forgetting—that ordinarily segregates contrary emotional states under the rule of dissociation.

My receptivity to and agreement with Dr. Bergson is intrinsic to my own position, that of conservative Judaism, which takes its stand on the chain of Tradition continued unbroken from Moses, yet welcomes continuous development, and opens the word of God to the spirit of the times. My disagreement with Dr. Bergson's characterization of Kafka's religious thought is likewise grounded in my position, but this is not a fertile conflict because it does not engage him in the area of his strength; it is a side issue for him, but not for me, and therefore merely a place for us to acknowledge our differences. However, my disagreement with Adrienne Gottbaum is of another kind entirely; it comes from the heart of my belief and goes to the heart of her argument. A stale argument, something we heard done to death years ago when cultural studies were in fashion: it is the all-too-familiar attempt to enclose Kafka in a narrow ideological position.

Only a few people got to hear her presentation—

we had to reschedule it as an early morning session due to the bad weather. I was there, and I was saddened and dismayed that those who were also there seemed taken in by loose associations spun into a web of distortions. Later, in the cafeteria during the lunch break, I heard them talking excitedly to colleagues about Ms. Gottbaum's critique of the conference, the buzz got around, until everywhere I went I heard people discussing it. So I can't let her argument go unanswered.

Ms. Gottbaum, a Yiddish folksinger whose mastery of her own field is indisputable, has set up shop as an independent scholar. She plays enticingly with Kafka's imagery, but when you look through her rhetorical performance—her displays of Benjaminian dialectical juggling—the thing she's aiming at clearly comes into focus: she takes Kafka's "ambivalence" and "hatred" as her theme. She wants to lift these concepts out from behind the veil under which they have been supposedly mystified by the other presenters. The move from "ambivalence" to "hatred" exposes the tendentious aspect of her work: she pushes valid arguments too far, so that Kafka appears to occupy her position. It's true that the conflict between "hatred" and "devotion" tormented Kafka, but Ms. Gottbaum at her most reductive makes it seem that hatred was the more vital motive, that it played a greater part in determining his development and artistic practice. At her most confused and confusing, she mashes up the antithetical elements in him, and emphasizes the destructive force at the expense of the glimpse of transcendence that Kafka attains in the area of his ambivalence, that is to say, his sphere of spiritual battle.

Let us examine two quotations that Ms. Gottbaum puts forward as evidence of Kafka's politics. In his biography of Kafka, Brod writes that Kafka once said to him, "How strange these workmen are. I am amazed at their modesty. Instead of storming the Institute and smashing it to pieces, they come and plead."[1] And Gustav Janouch, in his book *Conversations with Kafka*, reports how Kafka resolved the ethical dilemma that confronted him on the job: "where he felt that workers had been victimized by bureaucratic excesses, he surreptitiously sabotaged the Institute's case in court, on occasion even going to far as to pay the plaintiff's legal expenses."[2] Janouch has been discredited as a reliable witness; he cribbed some of the conversations that he claims to have had with Kafka from other sources; and no other source corroborates his statement about Kafka's covert acts of conscience. But let us put all that aside and assume for the sake of argument that Kafka told his young protégé something he revealed to no one else. The point I want to make, immediately, is that here we meet, not the closet revolutionary, but the Prague Jew.

For Janouch, as for Brod, Kafka's greatness as a writer was connected with his nobility of character. Janouch's book is the tribute of a grateful young poet to a master who took an interest in his development. It is quite credible that, in taking on the role of exemplar, Kafka divulged to Janouch, and to Janouch alone, his hidden act of charity. Jewish Tradition— it's folklore, literature and Scripture—knows this gesture by many names. The *Lamed Vavnik* is a figure of the hiddenness of the good deed, the essential deed, the world-sustaining deed. And Brontshe Shveyg is a figure of the saintliness of the unassuming worker.

There is less irony in Kafka's remark to Brod than amazement at the way of the world, or, if we must speak of irony, it is the naive irony of saintliness. The illumination comes with the word "modesty." How odd a word! In it all of Kafka's identification with the injured workmen is contained, an identification that combines sexual shyness and social inhibition so great that, according to Brod, he never talked when they were among a group of their friends. Acute self-consciousness and timidity enabled Kafka to empathize with the workers' mute sense of inferiority in the presence of powerful men. Kafka, when asked his politics, said simply that he was of "the party of the personnel."[3]

This sympathy with the underdog, this naive or saintly irony, this kindness, this sense of the morality of the workers' supposed nonviolence, tinged as it is for Kafka with pathos and a goodness that transcends the world of retaliation—this is the stuff that Jewish dialogue is made of, including secularized Jewish dialogue, with its long memory of "the other world," its inheritance of the prophetic Tradition which founded the spiritual kingdom on the pursuit of truth and justice. What we have here are not political fulminations and pronouncements, but fragments of the great dialogical fervor of the Jew of Mitteleuropa who looked on life with compassion and clear-eyed knowledge of human injustice.

In this light, Ms. Gottbaum's paper can be seen for what it is: a polemical attempt to rewrite Kafka from a narrow sectarian perspective. It is my conviction that Kafka's solidarity with his fellow man can best be understood from the purview, not of politics, but of religion. In this debate between a sociopolitical interpreter of the Kafka canon and one who views his work from a spiritual perspective, I want to give Kafka himself the last word. And so I close with this quotation from the theological reflections that Kafka wrote while convalescing in Zurau: "Humility provides everyone, even him who despairs in solitude, with the strongest relationship to his fellow man, and this immediately, though, of course, only in the case of complete and permanent humility. It can do this because it is the true language of prayer, at once adoration and the firmest of unions. The relationship to one's fellow man is the relationship of prayer, the relationship to oneself is the relationship of striving; it is from prayer that one draws the strength for one's striving."[4]

Notes

1. Max Brod, *Franz Kafka: A Biography*, translated by C. Humphreys Roberts and Richard Winston (New York: Schocken Books, 1963), 82. Hereafter *Kafka: A Biography.*
2. This is Pawel's summary of Janouch's discussion of Kafka's "saintliness" and "kindness" toward workers. See Ernst Pawel, *The Nightmare of Reason: A Life of Franz Kafka* (New York: The Noonday Press, 1984), 188. Also see Gustav Janouch, *Conversations with Kafka*, translated by Goronwy Rees (New York: A New Directions Book, 1971), 65-67.
3. *Kafka: A Biography*, 72
4. Franz Kafka, *The Blue Octavo Notebooks*, translated by Ernst Kaiser and Eithne Wilkins (Cambridge: Exact Change, 1991), 91.

V. DISAPPEARING ACTS

The longer aphorisms as well as the narrative pieces [refract] the dialogue of the divided soul in which one part is whipped by anxiety and the other [is] meditatively yearning for peace; but it is in the nature of the dialogue that the lines of argument are not clearly drawn, that one argument serves as the distorting mirror of the other, so that the result is neither an antithesis nor a synthesis, but an encounter in a labyrinth. The labyrinth, like all such mythological configurations, is an obstacle barricading a center. In Kafka's case, this center is believed to be there, but impossible of access; at best, it can only be glimpsed in the extreme vanishing point of distance.... Thus it remains true that art and truth cannot coincide because they belong to different orders of being; the truth can be apprehended only by spirit but not encompassed by words, which can capture only the reflection of its grotesque trace of truth as the point of disappearance.

    —Walter A. Strauss, "Trying to Mend the Broken
      Vessels," in *Kafka's Contextuality*

37. In Kafka's Labyrinth
Adrienne Gottbaum, M.A.*

From: Adrienne Gottbaum [mailto: adrienneyiddishsong@
goldenhorn.com]

To: alappel@dharmaseed.com, dsBeagle@m&a.edu,
tomrcole@msn.com, philfried@aol.com, dmetzger@gmail.com
nurkseD@verizon.net, markweiss@artscroll.com, suewillis@
earthlink.net, pzimet@talkingband.org, eileenwiseman@
lovethyneighbor.org
Sent: October 11, 2024 at 6:08 PM
Subject: My Censored Paper

Dear Friends:
Thank you for your encouragement and ongoing interest in
my Kafka project. Here are excerpts from the paper that Bryk
refused to publish in the volume of conference papers that he
edited. In his concluding remarks, without being able to bring
himself to utter the s-word, he focused his repudiation of my
work on what he called my narrow ideological position. I did
mention in passing that Kafka occasionally attended socialist
meetings in the evening, but he never spoke at these meetings,
or of them, and I suggested that a combination of restlessness
on a night when he couldn't write, hunger for community,
curiosity, and solidarity with the underdog drew him to these

*Adrienne Gottbaum, M.A., was renowned in the world of Yiddish as a
teacher and performer of Yiddish folk song. The former Associate Director
of the YIVO Institute for Jewish Research, she left her position to devote
herself full-time to her career as a singer and independent scholar. She became
interested in Kafka while researching *Hot Jews: The Yiddish Stage in Kafka's
Life and Work*, unfinished at the time of her sudden death, will be published
posthumously in 2029 by YIVO and Northwestern University Press.

meetings. (It must be remembered that socialism was a mass sentiment in the early twentieth century, a view shared by many people for whom it never amounted to anything so definite as a political commitment.) (Kafka was an avid reader of newspapers, and no doubt it was the same interest in the events of his day that drew him to these meetings.) But this is incidental to my overall critique of the ideological project of the Kafka conference on "the bureaucrat as artist," and, in response to your questions, I am sending you the excerpts that restore Kafka to the labyrinth in which he eluded the identities that were constructed for him, and disappeared into the black hole that permanently absorbed him.

Declaration / Concealment

At 21, in his famous letter to Oskar Pollak, Kafka writes his credo, and, at the same time, intimates and conceals what he needs, under the sign of the ax. "What we need are books that hit us like a most painful misfortune, like the death of someone we loved more than we love ourselves, that make us feel as though we had been banished to the woods, far from any human presence, like a suicide. A book must be the ax for the frozen sea within us. That is what I believe." No sign remains of the forbidden intimacy he craved except the intense negativity of the image under which he expresses his longing. And he speaks of his absolute sense of vocation evasively, not as a writer but as a reader of books; the two are, of course, inseparable, and the latter passes over into the former in any actual writing practice. As in a dream, Kafka condenses his need for Pollak's love and his love of writing into an image that fuses them into a shock whose sources remain hidden as long as what we read "doesn't shake us awake like a blow to the skull." Pollak must have been struck by the image, and even felt its reverberations pass through his body, without understanding a word of what he read.

Envelope of Invisibility

As a child, Kafka encountered his father's power with two defenses: frozenness and hiddenness. These two things rolled into a single overwhelming process. He shrank into himself, became numb, and disappeared. At an early age, he already had a well-developed sense of invisibility, his own invisibility in the physical world ruled by his father. But he lived in constant danger because some part of him might be seized by an impulse, withdrawn from his control, and brought to his father's attention, as when he thrust his hand violently into a wash basin, splattering the water, or thrust out his lower jaw as he had seen a boxer square his round face on entering the ring, a piece of mimicry of which he hadn't been quite aware, until his father roared, "And now you're pretending to be an ape?" By the time he recited his Haftorah portion by rote at the lectern of his father's synagogue, he was better able to keep everything that surged through him under his surveillance, which strengthened his capacity to keep even extreme emotion under strict control. To this he added his dervishlike capacity for spinning without losing his balance, spinning around and collecting intelligence on what was happening on all sides of his body as well as inside his head. As a Jew, as a closeted gay man, as a writer, he lived in hiding; but in each precinct of his shame and guilt, he grew as a mole, a great mole who sneaked and sniffed around the corridors to which he had privileged access, making elaborate notes on how the humans there lived, paying particular attention to the theatrical gestures by which they gave away things that they did not or could not verbalize.

139

He discovered a second language, and another way of telling stories, at the Yiddish theater, where he was overwhelmed by the gesticulations of the actors; they cut through his habitual reserve, had him doubled up in laughter, and drew tears whose salt taste in his mouth felt like the initiation he hadn't experienced at his bar mitzvah. Out of the counterpoint between the German language and the Yiddish gestures—extravagant bits of buffoonery or impetuous acts that were wildly out of place—he fashioned the work of his maturity. The eruption of physical gestures onto the pages he wrote dramatized an Elsewhere beyond the ken of the verbal surface, inserting a gap between the words and a locus of meanings that remained unsaid but that undermined the semantic authority of the German.

With this breakthrough, Kafka opened the way toward what Deleuze and Guattari call "a minor literature," by which they mean: a literature that invents techniques to disrupt the seemlessness (sic) of a major language and imparts to it something hitherto unformulated, the collective experience of a minority group "forced to serve" a language not its own. In one of the late stories, an investigating dog remembers the troupe of seven singing dogs dancing on their hind legs that raised his consciousness up to the airborne food that descended from a mysterious source; in his last story, a voice in the first person plural, speaking on behalf of the mouse-folk, commemorates the *khazonish* diva, Josephine, who gave her congregational audience a sense of refuge in times of danger by singing their common fear and happiness in a voice no different than their own. In these stories, Kafka is remembering the impact on him of Leyvi's Yiddish actors at the Café Savoy, and writing his way toward Yiddish literature in the German.

As Punishment

We have had many Kafkas: the religious allegorist, the Oedipal author, the social prophet who foretold the everyday life of totalitarianism, the great novelist of the age of anxiety, the fabulist who wrote coded narratives on the Jewish question, the closeted queer poet, the man who turned himself into a writing machine to disassemble the prison-house of organicist language, that is, the deconstructionist *avant la lettre*. The organizers of this conference now propose that we take up Kafka under yet another idea, that we in our presentations and discussions collaborate in establishing Kafka's identity in terms of the bureaucrat as artist, as if such a Kafka might serve as a real and substantial exemplar for our time of mass unemployment and meaningless work.

Kafka forged an ax with which to break out of such constructions; it didn't split things into true or false. His vocation as a writer and his job as an office worker did and did not exist in antithetical relation to each other, they mutually interpenetrated, informed and shaped each other, they also supported each other, not simply with the complementarity under which the conference organizers wish to enclose and unify them, but under the law that simultaneously tore Kafka apart and allowed him to go on doing as he liked. Office work was the toll he paid by day for the freedom of movement he claimed as his right at night when everyone else was asleep.

The Clash of Battle

Kafka's ax is a logic-chopping instrument that takes down all certitude, and it is a loosely associative process that defies the logic of any single code or system. It entered his lexicon as a sign of his vocation as a reader and writer of a supreme book, a book that could cut through his deadness and allow him to feel the oceanic life within. After his encounter with Yiddishkeit, the ax turned into something else, something different, a sign of the livelihood that permitted him to safeguard his writing from the demands of the day, the stain of living in the world. Nevertheless, his life as a bourgeois, an office worker, wasn't simply camouflage, a false self covering and protecting a true one; the compliant and disobedient selves could not be integrated or finally dissociated from each other; they were each there to return the other to the dark where he listened hard but couldn't see what he heard. Was it the clash of battle-axes? Metaphors arose to fill the void, he wanted no part of them, but they were all he had with which to fight on in the dark. Kafka's ax, insofar as it was a metaphor of self, was two-headed, had a cutting edge in back of each of its heads, faced forward into the past, backward into the future, cut through time to reveal the eternity in which all his striving was futile.

The Two-Headed Ax

At the time he wrote to Pollak, Kafka believed he was

a naturalized citizen of the republic of Western letters, Goethe was his god, he had traveled widely in the classics and traced his heritage back to the ancient Greeks. If you read him boldly, applying his own method of imaginative inquiry, following whatever image seized him to wherever it led, accepting associations that fall outside one's usual conception of the object as keys to its character, you find the ax taking you back to the palace of Knossos, where the earliest examples of the labrys or two-headed ax were uncovered. Everywhere an intruder into the palace turned, there it was, carved on the walls of its 1300 rooms, built around a central courtyard, and on the walls of corridors of varying sizes and directions that made it impossible for any but the initiated to move from room to room without getting lost; anyone who came to find and kill the King quickly found himself trapped. Not only were images of the labrys found decorating the living quarters of the palace, but the tool itself was found in great abundance and in many variations in the storerooms reached through subterranean passages under the palace proper. Kafka, I believe, would have drawn it out of his own imagination if he hadn't found it ready-made in the ancient world. For the Greeks who invented it, the symbolic function of the labrys exceeded and displaced its practical use as a weapon or a tool for cutting, splitting, and shaping wood. Its doubleness rendered it metonymic, and, as a metonym, it slipped through the contiguous but divided cities of the Peloponnesus and became the sign of their common culture: its very multiplicity made it usable as the dominant emblem of their civilization. With no fixed form or meaning, its two heads might be left bare or elaborately decorated with inlaid patterns, and it ranged in size from small hand-held ceremonial objects to holy tools taller than the priests who wielded them to slaughter bulls for sacrifice to the gods. First associated with the female divinities who ruled the ebbs and flows of oceans and fates, it was taken over by the young male storm-gods, and ended as the exclusive possession of Zeus, who sits enthroned in temples throughout Hellas with the triple thunderbolt in one hand and the double ax in the other. Labyrinthos, the Greek for labyrinth, is derived from the word labrys.

Exodus

Somewhere in his writings, Kafka speaks of the Sinai as "the desert labyrinth." At the moment of reading it, I didn't mark the passage for later use. As often happens with a phrase of Kafka's, it returned long afterward, when I could no longer recover its source, but I could feel the impact that it had made on me, the imperishable impact that flooded through me the first time when I was too swept away by the passage to take notes on it. My note-taking allows me to forget the too-much of my reading, whereas this phrase entered the archive of indestructible memory from which it returned as an archetype, as the origin and goal of the following trail of associations:

In Kafka's pages, the ax-head flies off the handle and leaves the forests of Eastern Europe where it was used by peasants hired by Jewish lumber merchants such as my great-grandfather Barukh to farm the hard wood for the landed gentry. Estranged from its origins, it becomes a metaphor, and not one metaphor, but several, yet they are alike in this: Kafka's metaphors aspire to the condition of metonymies, in which their association with things is based on contiguity rather than similarity. His key images, once they have started on their flight from resemblance, go on to desert every single symbol system to which they momentarily appear to belong. The labyrinth, associated with the double-headed ax in the foundational language of Western thought, enters the Jewish register of his writing as a trackless waste, a labyrinth that has no physical form, no visible walls or paths, a labyrinth that a small people, hobbled by centuries of enslavement, inscribes in the sand with their feet by going around in circles in the desert.

No Exit

In one of its aspects, the labrys signifies the artifice of
Daedelus, who designed the labyrinth of Knossos to
imprison and hide the monstrous creature begotten by the
Queen of Crete and the Bull from the Sea. This suggests a
certain parallel between the mythological Greek artist and
the labyrinths constructed by the modern Jewish novelist
for his mole, his ape, his dog, his mice, but this parallel is
misleading; it trails off into senseless paths that reproduce
the labyrinth out-of-doors. In Kafka's speculative narratives,
there is no Ariadne, no thread that holds from beginning to
end, no way out.

Kafka: Artist and Bureaucrat

He is a mole engaged in surveillance of the powers among
whom he is forced by circumstance to live and work. Only
Dr. Bergson acknowledges Kafka's "hostility" to the Institute,
but he does so to bring out all the more poignantly Kafka's
achievement in going beyond his hatred and self-division,
and writing passages in which a sense of sublime depth is
attained by mixing contrary emotional states. In Kafka,
sublimation, such as it was, entailed his achievement of
ambivalence rather than his transcendence of hatred and self-
division, an achievement that came through burrowing down
rather than rising up—an achievement that was episodic,
but that he went on developing by placing his life in the
service of his art as absolutely as the hasidim of Ger served
God. His days at the office, his nights of writing hinged
on his discipline; together they forge the fruitful impasse,
the necessary abyss, which was the optimal condition for
his discipline to flourish. The day that subtracted time and
energy from the night called upon him to make fearful

efforts to write, his devotion drew strength from his hatred, his hatred from his devotion, a hateful devotion, a devoted hatred ran through his nights as it ran through his days, destroying as it created, creating as it destroyed.

38. Independent Scrutiny

In the cutting-edge factories, he observes
the operation of blades that whirl 4000 turns
a minute, the kickback of the wood
can neither be foreseen nor prevented
when the wood is knotted or warped
or the blade isn't fast enough
or the pressure of the hand is uneven,
such inevitable mischances
don't pass without several joints
or whole fingers cut off.

*

It's not my job to visit the men
in hospital, but I go.
Men grown silent with
no one to hear their complaints.
Bodies mutilated and wasting away.
How could I not go?

*

Almost day, Joseph K. appears
before me: he hears convulsive sighs
behind a door, tears it open and discovers
a lumber room in the bank
along the corridor between his office
and the staircase, there he sees
two underlings entirely delivered

into the power of a third
man, who is sheathed
in a leather garment that leaves
his arms and chest bare,
he orders the men to strip
and with a practiced hand proceeds
to mark their flesh with his birch rod.

*

With a pencil and a blue
octavo notebook, he takes up his own
hazardous occupation. Anyone
who can't come to terms with his life
needs one hand to ward off
a little of his despair
while with the other hand he
notes down what he sees
among the ruins because he sees more
and different things than the others, chained
by necessity to concrete tasks.

Dead as he is in his own
lifetime, he alone is granted a second
life of sorts that frees
him coolly
to survey the daily costs
of laboring in the pain factories

unless he needs both or more
hands than he's been given
in this fight with despair.

39. Reflection in a Jewish Shopwindow

Spent all afternoon in the streets, bathing in Jew-hatred. Crowds hunting their prey with stones and clubs, screaming, "Filthy rabble." Max, stern-faced, absolutely pedagogical in his anger at me: You must promise me, etc.

But I slipped by unnoticed, I've come to count on my invisibility.

From a third-story window, Max saw a bearded man of his acquaintance—not Jewish, but obese, taken as a Jew—being beaten.

Don't you see? You proved my point. Being so thin, I passed through the eye of their prejudice.

No, you're not exempt, you feel it too—the anxiety of being noticed. And the bearded man, what happened to him?

The riot squad dispersed the mob, he lived. But you—I don't understand what possessed you to go down there.

Fascination and hatred. The counteroffensive against the shame of having to live under police protection. The heroism of the cockroach, which also won't be driven out of the bathroom.

A man shuffling along from one wall to the next, pressing himself against it as if looking for a soft spot where the wall will yield and let him pass through. The fear, always, of taking up too much room. That's how you know he's Jewish. For his neighbors, he's still walking down their street with too much pushiness. Or else, why these hammer blows against his body, at irregular intervals?

This blood has washed away Max's doubts about
Zionism. I remind him that, until these latest incidents, he
was fond of saying that no one with any self-esteem engages
in politics. But self-esteem never stood between me and
anything.

A long thin
creature with
a friendly
smile in the
plate-glass
of my father's
store, now
as always, he
doesn't seem
there, smiling
out of shame
and fear, yet
he looks back
at me with a
raptor's gaze
and his skull
is supplied
with a surplus
of lustrous hair,
his neighbors
must also be-
lieve he has
a soul which
clings to life
in the image
and that his

lineaments are
sequestered
in the memory
of mirrors, so
to efface every
trace of my 38
Jewish years
they will smash
this window.

40. The Descent

He looked down, concentrated, took small steps, so as not to step on cracks that marked the precipice separating him from his nearest friend.

Brod put one foot in front of the other as if it were inconceivable that the crowd wouldn't part to let him through.

But for Kafka the way was closed: he saw the impenetrable outline of every human body moving toward him and it was horrible.

As they walked side-by-side in their different worlds, he told Brod that he hadn't completely evolved as a man because he belonged to a porous species that had once lived in perfect symbiosis with every living thing in Paradise. What he remembered most was the moment when he was personally expelled from the Garden. Around the angel who barred the way back, a gate appeared where there had been no gate, and he remained stuck there, in the shock of it.

In his long walks with Brod, he was merely pacing back and forth at a threshold he couldn't cross.

Sometimes when he was away from paper, he forgot where he was and entered a time of exaltation; animals came through and uttered themselves word for word in German. Later, he blindly and arbitrarily snatched handfuls out of the living stream, but his near-verbatim acquisition was nothing compared to the fullness in which they lived. He was incapable of restoring that fullness.

Of the Kafkan creatures who were not written down, one survives because it began as a glimpse of something which he told Brod when they were out walking, but it turned as he talked into a bizarre hybrid, part-angel, part-bat; it was too late for him to take it back into the silence where such beings came to term.

If the poet couldn't carry his parables across the lost stream, imagine how much less lives on in the version that Brod told to Yitzkhok Leyvi, who added it to his repertoire; it was among the monologues he performed in the poor theaters of the Warsaw ghetto.

"Imagine," Yitzkhok Leyvi told his audiences, "that we are in the old Prague ghetto. In this piece I play Max Brod, and my companion, the person I'm talking to, is my real-life self, Yitzkhok Leyvi, who, like me, is a living archive and disseminator of Kafka's sayings and parables." The lights went out for a moment, then came back on, and the actor portraying Brod and the invisible figure of Yitzkhok Leyvi were seen walking around the streets of the ghetto at a brisk pace as Brod gave over the story that Kafka had told him:

"The ascent of man, Kafka said, was the material process that revealed a corresponding descent of angels. He could see them, he said, mutilated by being battered against human thresholds, which got harder and more narrow the more every tribe built up its borders. This made the angels desperate, they tried throwing themselves through cracks in great walls, they had their pinions shorn off by ritual fences woven of razor-sharp distinctions; prohibitions constricted the holes they wished to pass through, given them teeth. Over millennia, through this process of scarring, they lost invisibility by degrees; the surfaces of their bodies were marked with gashes, welts, bites; they became gross, too broken to call upon prophets who waited for them at gates where nothing but screeching shadows flitted by."

The tattoo of the actor's feet on the creaking floorboards, which accompanied this speech, was underscored when he suddenly stopped pacing and faced the audience. He looked down, concentrated, and, when he resumed walking, took small steps. He spoke so softly that the audience had to strain to hear him. They quickly realized that he was now Kafka, speaking directly to them. As he spoke, the lights in the darkened cabaret came on, and the dimmed spotlights were gradually raised, erasing the difference between the small, bare stage and the crowded room under the hard, common light of day.

"In the world below, the angels had become unrecognizable. Even then, they didn't give up striving to be with their chosen ones. This is what defeated them, this selection of a single species through whom to carry on a dialogue between heaven and earth. And even when the angels knew their misfortune—it was a consequence of their original fault, their submission to the Law that granted the creature they called Man dominion over all living things— they nonetheless persisted, because they couldn't go on being angels without humans who saw them among mountains and received them in valleys and adored them in set-apart places, homes and temples. Even as they saw that they were destroying themselves, they went on, determined to break into armories that walked around on two legs, until, blackened by their coagulated blood (so greatly had their substance been altered through contact with us), they became bats that survived blindly, guided by their own echoes at night and hanging upside down by day, shrieking in human attics and spires."

41. WALKING AROUND

I'm tired of walking around
as a man, walking
into the office
of the man who grants you a safe conduct
to enter the chambers of the higher-up
who passes you
on to the next interrogation
where you earn the right
to walk around as a man.

*

Beggars wearing the guise
of peddlers, cans of pencils
tied to their necks, they bark
well-rehearsed speeches, they show
a full set of stumps or a few sliced-off
fingers to pierce
the story you walk around
inside of, which blames them
for failing to pass
the exams that permit
certain mammals from the inferior
races and lower orders
to attain the status of persons.

*

Under the table, pigeons march within inches of our chairs,
puff up their feathers, hesitate, advance a step, retreat, charge

a morsel, scoff it down, fly off at top speed, return for the
next raid. We sit above them, sipping coffee, and enjoying
our sachertorte. Yitzkhok Leyvi shows up and coos, Ah, the
doves, doves all around us! Max falls in with his mood. On the
ground they move like wind-up dolls, but the moment they
stretch their wings and soar—what beauty! They would lift
our hearts to the heavens, if only we let them. I think, They're
the sort of people who think the human species is a good idea.
But I'm not exempt from the fever that cooks their brains. We
watch pigeons struggle for every bit of food they snatch from
the gutter, and think them blessed. We envy their innocence,
we succumb to the temptation to turn them into metaphors
in our wish to escape the violence that spoils our pleasure.
Because to permit someone to starve in public is, after all,
violence. And to see these filthy city birds as messengers of a
higher world is another act of violence which clouds our gaze.
Driven by our hunger for blessings.

*

You never speak
to them, never
sit down beside them
and say that you're tired
of the six-foot frame
that's too tall for you
to carry past them,
but if you let yourself
stop alongside them
and rest,
you'd never get up,
all you can do is
buy your pencils from them.

*

Write down what you cannot
say on every street and corridor
that leads to the chambers of
the man who can dictate
whether you stand or sit:
he can strike
whole days from your calendar,
he keeps you from taking care
of your real affairs,
which you do alone, at night,
in secret, a mole
too possessed of animal pride
to sink to your knees
and beg for a renewal
of your human visa.

*

I'm tired of my parables.
When they don't work,
I feel dead. When they do,
they ferry me across to the real life
I'm too weak to carry on,
the fatigue no end
of writing will mitigate, the sign
of the change my body is
dying for. My spine
wasn't designed for this
performance—having to pretend
that for me it's not a terrible strain
to walk around on my hind legs.

42. Household God

For every man in pain
his particular god,
for the tubercular, the god of suffocation

whom I created
through twenty years
of painstaking labor

who grew wise
as I proceeded never to learn
anything useful

who succeeded
me along the path
of my long retreat

and camped
among the graves
of my failures

in an unbuttoned
greatcoat, gaining
patience

as he watched
me stop my race
against time all night

in my ecstasy
but lose it every day
at sunrise.

*

I vowed
to put myself out
of reach of my father's idols

eliminated small
pleasures, allowed myself
to become a physical
wreck

while the god
of my writing feasted
on my abstinence until
he was thick

enough to show himself
in my room, he leapt
onto my bed and sat
on my chest

and rode me toward the goal
where I wouldn't have to
struggle with him
for a breath.

*

I was too weak
to resist the good
fortune

that life bestows
with so many careless
gifts on the healthy man

as if despair
and illness weren't as great
a distraction, nonetheless

of the two ways of choking
off the writing, I erred
on the side of the weightier god.

43. THE OTHER HAND

Two laws work
together to destroy him:
the Jewish one ("a man without

a woman is not
a human being"),
and the law of the ax ("cut

out any impure thing"),
a monkish taboo, a desire
for the contemplative life (the Christian

one) has him walking around all winter
in a summer suit, and fasting as the supreme
instrument of his investigations.

As he grows lighter, he begins
to see a seat reserved for him
in the world above,

and it is the same
place where he is chained
to his desk in the world below,

but in heaven, he unrolls
a scroll in whose white
spaces he finds a flamelike

script for the infinite
story he goes on writing,
while in hell, he clings

to a rod of Torah
with which he goes on beating what's left
of the hand that writes.

44. SERVING THE EVIL ONE

Writing is a sweet and marvelous reward—
but for what?

*

Lights out at eleven,
the house is quiet, dress
in a freshly ironed shirt,
sit down at the desk and begin again.

*

During the course of the night it comes to me—
a reward for serving the Evil One.

*

This regimen serves me well.
In the afternoon when everyone's banging
pots against stovetops, doorposts, and my forehead,
I slip between my sheets and take
a three-hour nap.

This descent to the dark powers,
unleashing ghosts that are kept bound during office hours,
those questionable embraces and who knows what else
may be going on down there—

none of it is remembered as one writes
in the well-lit room above.

This is my method. There may be other ways
of writing. I know only this one.
At night when fear keeps me
from sleeping, only this one.

45. An Incurable Condition

Days of Awe

He awoke into the patchy
uptake above his headboard
and knew it was the refusal of his dream
to disperse into the day.
He had done the thing forbidden
to him: respected the letter
of the Law separating his livelihood

from his writing while infiltrating its spirit
with his spite, his frustration, his failure
to let his pursuit of truth and justice end
in forgiveness. How could he soar
when the deeds of his right hand were undone
by his left, which clutched
the ax he couldn't bury?

In bed with a cloud
of gray matter under which he had trouble
breathing, he saw
that if for him the gates were to open,
he would demand the right
to be despairing in heaven
as he was on earth.

And He Confessed to His Diary

Surely there were others who preferred what they did for
themselves alone in bed to exchanging fluids with someone
else's body. It was only natural, even our ancestors the great
apes masturbated.

In the Burning Lucidity of his Stories

He could think of nothing but torturing himself and others.
This was the conversation he could have with no one else; it
inspired him to reveal the true love to which he pled guilty
in the grip of the torture-machine he invented in his stories;
it was the source of his being peculiarly stained, a stain that
induced a loneliness so great he was afraid it would make him
go mad. But no—he found a self-cure for his madness in the
burning lucidity of his stories. The work of living and writing
his damnation saved him.

Proof

How could he be proof
against the myth of redemption
when his sense of sin
was more real to him
than his own right hand?

46. The Book of Misfortune

He was sitting and waiting
at a long table in the otherwise
empty library of the Lord,

just as he nodded off
the man whose coat made him appear
broader than he was

returned from the stacks
carrying the book he needed
to look into, but the ordeal

had only begun, after every few
steps the man had to put the book
down, it was as tall as himself

and heavy, a thick volume
of parchment bound in leather
and sealed with iron clasps,

he took it up again, moved it
forward, rested, his trip
across the room exhausted him,

but the man did reach him
and heave the book onto the table
and open it and point to the line

where his name was inscribed
under the sentence, "Know
that the judgment of your life

is your life," then shut
the book and left him
alone in the monumental room,

bereft and wretched, reading
his fate in the wreck
he had let himself become.

*

That his self-preoccupation
had earned him a permanent place
in the library where he passed

his time on earth, reading
that the future which awaited him
had already happened.

*

That he would remain sensitive
to the slightest noise, odor, change
of atmospheric pressure,

that Sundays or crossing the Alps
on his first day of vacation would be bad
as his first day back at the office,

that these things would set off the aura
of a migraine that would last
beyond his own lifetime.

*

That ideas would come thick
as flies, copulate in his palm,
with a clap he would gather them,
pin them to the page

with periods, his eyes
on fire, ice wrapped in a towel
around his temples, crowned
by thundering light.

*

That he would never see the holy text
thaw into four great rivers
that were said to run from Paradise,

that for him there would be no
sources of renewal
in which to immerse himself,

that he would never be
restored to simple and loyal
community with his people,

that he did not desire a place
at their holiday table
more than lucidity,

that he would find no one
to whom he could make known the powers
against which he was powerless,

that he was a traitor
whether he broke his silence
or failed to speak,

that he disfigured—so as to hide
even from himself—the revelations
stored up in him,

that each moment he remained alive
he compounded his offense, mounted
waste upon waste.

47. FUTURE OF THE TEXT

Dear Milena, you hear the German
vowels, half-strangled by the consonants
that surround them, laboring for breath,
a paper language brought to life
by an irregular rasp, a slight gasp, sudden
squeaks destroy the words' silencing
of the noises they make in their rush
toward sense, the music of the work
is just this struggle to burst out
of constricting forms, you bear it
into the Czech with perfect pitch.

Beloved translator, the author of those
stories sends you his thanks, amazed
at how faithful you are to his death
in the text: you follow his endless
sentences to an impossible theater
of operations: a Jew addressing
his audience in a borrowed language,
he takes an inventory of the clothes
he strips from his body, lays
himself out and summons his last
strength to make a final report
of the cuts that killed him
as he performs an autopsy
on his own corpse just before
it stopped stifling its horrible cries.

48. The Pigeon

In this scene, Kafka crawls
into bed, his every tendon craves
sleep, yet his gaze flits
back to the wood-burning

stove, he watches tongues
of fire licking the logs
and hissing against
the damp spots,

he can't black
out the orgy
of metaphors that come
between him and the flames,

he sits back up, lifts his
attention out of the trance
that's consumed his existence
and narrates the fire:

"Everything I saw appeared constructed,
I chased after constructions, I walked
into a room, and there they were,
in a corner, a bright tangle"—

he wants to pursue
this, but a pigeon
lands on his windowsill
and clucks without letup.

*

Have you never listened
to a pigeon? They don't cluck
and their cooing never
invited me on a voyage.

City boy, Jew, you
want me to reappear
and speak to your Kafka
project and I will.

You still pine for
music that would bring news
from the sky. That noise
at the window—I don't know

how you could mistake it
for an urban dove—listen
hard—tiny thuds
against glass—that's no bird—

it's an insect, separated
from the out-of-doors
with its dung and flowers, flying
a suicidal mission against

the windowpane, in the hope
of being restored to the world
that's become, during a brief
absence, paradise.

49. WHITE SPACES

while writing
       his hand flying across the page
              leaves his body
back
       in the signifying factory
              that reproduces the world
in which the hand remains attached
       to the shoulder
              so he can't fly
into the white
       spaces he creates—
              breaking
down the chains of attachment

VI. THE KAFKAN SENTENCE

Here, for once, a world is expressed in which redemption cannot be anticipated—go and explain this to the goyim! I believe that at this point your critique will become just as esoteric as its subject; the light of revelation never shone as unmercifully as it does here.

—Gershom Scholem,
from the correspondence with Walter Benjamin
on Kafka's work, *Walter Benjamin: The Story of a Friendship*

50. The Wood-Burning Stove

Forty years ago, before computers speeded up the worldwide destruction of memory culture, Adrienne Gottbaum came to see me, seeking access to the Jewish nursing homes where I'd organized reminiscence groups, memoir-writing workshops, and intergenerational oral history projects. She was particularly interested in obtaining a letter of introduction to Judah Palevsky, gatekeeper at the Hebrew Actors' Home, where she hoped to find actors who had worked with or known Kafka's friend, Yitzkhok Leyvi. She hoped that among the tens of thousands of elderly immigrants and survivors in New York, there had to be at least a few who had seen Leyvi's company or his solo performances in the cities and small towns of Eastern and Western Europe. I gave her eighteen variants of the same letter, each personally addressed to the administrator of an institution where she sought to pursue her project.

This was when I first heard about *Heyse Yidn*, the book she planned to write about Kafka. "*Heyse yidn*," literally "hot Jews," originally meant Hasidic Jews on fire with their faith or the ultra-Orthodox Talmudists who opposed them, exceedingly pious rabbinic scholars like Kafka's grandfather; but the term was later expanded to include secular Jews like Max Brod, Jews proud of their ancient tradition, and passionately committed to one or another of the modern Jewish movements—religious, political, philosophical or artistic—that flourished in modern times. In Adrienne's view, Kafka became a "*heyse yid*" during the years 1911 and 1912 when he spent his nights at the Yiddish theater. In his *Diaries*, he details his "steadfast love" for the actors and the plays. "Some of the songs, the expression '*yiddische kinderlach*,' the sight of this woman on the stage—who, because she is Jewish, attracts us spectators because we are Jewish, with no desire for Christians or interest in them—made my cheeks tremble." A far cry from the universalism of the assimilated Jew who didn't permit Jews to enter his novels and stories until they cast off the particularity of their origin. His dry sobbing washed away his indifference to everything Jewish and his disdain for the crude art of the music hall. Adrienne, given her intimacy with modern Yiddish culture, appreciated what others had missed or discussed with condescension. In two phrases, Kafka expressed his grasp of the source and meaning of these plays: "Stolen liturgical melodies. The whole people sings them." An ember of love and belonging that he hadn't known he carried burst into flame. A sudden longing and reverence for the Tradition about which, he now realized, he knew nothing. This transient passion had enduring results: it led to his lifelong study of Jewish history, rabbinic storytelling, Hebrew, and Torah, which he learned with Dora Diamont, the only woman he ever lived with.

Like Yitzkhok Leyvi, Dora Diamont had been raised in a Hasidic household; she, too, had broken away from it, yet her deepest feelings were stirred by people, causes and practices that evoked the sacred realm of her childhood. In her acts of devotion, her caring for orphans from the East in the Berlin Jewish Home, and for Kafka in the last months of his life, and for the revolution that would bring justice to the world, she lived in continuing contact with the messianic intensity of the heart that marked her as the daughter of Gerer hasidim. Kafka's feeling for everything pertaining to Judaism blew hot and cold over the years. Adrienne made an important contribution when she demonstrated that at one time or another traces of every major Jewish position appeared in his writing (Halakhic supremacy, Hasidism,

Haskalah, Zionism, Bundism, Yiddishism, Wissenschaft des Judentum). He imaginatively entertained the entire spectrum of Jewish life, but was not bound by any of the fixed positions that Jews fervently defended in their never-ending war of words. Despite a certain aloofness, an incapacity or refusal to embrace any doctrine, Kafka's interest in everything that might safeguard the Jewish future grew warm again in the last years of his life, and hot during the six months that he lived with Dora.

In the Yiddish theater, Adrienne said, the Jew and the artist came together. The plays summoned his detailed attention, and it was this, as he noted in his diary, that "concentrated my energy"; he left the theater ready to write. For Kafka, "attention is the natural prayer of the heart," the holy fire that he sought, early and late. From the fire of his youth to the fire of his last days—that's how Adrienne summarized the narrative arc of her book-project, whose point of departure was a passage in a letter that Walter Benjamin wrote to Gershom Scholem. "Kafka was far from the first to face [the breakdown of tradition]. Many had accommodated themselves to it, adhering to the truth or whatever they regarded as truth at any given moment and, with a more or less heavy heart, foregoing its transmissibility. Kafka's real genius is that he tried something new; he sacrificed truth for the sake of clinging to its transmissibility." In these few sentences, Adrienne said, Benjamin revealed why he found in Kafka an ancestor figure, as unlikely as this was, and as repugnant as it would have been to him to play any such part. Perpetually estranged from his own family and people, he was nonetheless one of the few Jews of his time through whom the midrashic inheritance passed into modernity. He was ever intent on his purpose, making a place in literature for the objects of his attention that preserve the aura of an indestructible mystery, even as it covers the roads of our world in confusion. "He is a great courage-teacher," Adrienne said. "Through him, I can believe what David sang of himself in the Psalms, namely, that the Lord wants to make use of broken vessels. This sustains me when I feel too small to carry out the task that gives me life." With a shudder, I saw her as the mouse-singer Josephine, through whom Kafka portrayed the pathos and transmissibility of the wordless melodies of the folk tradition.

*

Over the years, Adrienne visited me from time to time to tell me Kafka stories. My office at the Brookdale Center on Aging was bare and institutional, a gray desk, two gray file cabinets, a typewriter, two chairs, but it overlooked the East River and, if I closed the door and put up a "Do Not Disturb" sign, it offered complete privacy. Adrienne found this bureaucratic space just right for reading excerpts from her work-in-progress. The office was small and neutral, but it opened out onto a spectacular view of the bend in the river around the old neighborhood through which millions of immigrants had entered America. In reading fragments of Kafka's prose, she followed the cadence he had scored with his punctuation and she relied on the impact of his words, refraining from any impressive effects that she could have achieved with her magnificent contralto voice. Of course, I taped her—these were bravura performances. Later, in editing her unfinished work, I wove in some of what she spontaneously added as she read to me.

*

Into their unheated room at the edge of Berlin, Dora brought a spirit stove, which doubled as a hearth. After supper, she and Kafka huddled beside it. He shivered with pleasure as she told him stories about her escape from the closed world of her childhood; or she lay on the couch as he read Grimms' fairy tales or Kleist to her; or their hands danced in the air as they improvised shadow plays; or they dreamed of going to Palestine where they would open a café, he would be the waiter, she would be the cook; or they read a novel in Hebrew that didn't gloss over how depressing life really was in Jerusalem; or they learned Torah together, as the price of fuel soared, until an evening at their improvised hearth cost hundreds of thousands, then millions of marks. They cut back on alcohol for their lamp and used the spirit stove as their sole source of light and heat, but after a month of hyperinflation, even that became out of reach.

They didn't sit in the cold for long. Dora, endlessly resourceful, constructed something that looked like a hibachi out of a broken trough, with two sheets of ceiling tin for a base and chicken wire for a grill, parts that she purchased in a junk shop. She foraged in the streets for furniture left behind after an eviction, but rarely had luck, because no sooner were the contents of a neighbor's home set out on the curb, then other freezing hands snatched them and carried them off for fuel. So, with a concealed ax under her coat, she went off at dusk into the woods near their rented room—Steglitz, the outlying district where they lived, still looked like the village it had been before it was incorporated into Berlin—and brought back twigs, sticks and branches in her rucksack. It was illegal to have a wood-burning stove in their room, which wasn't vented, but she imagined that if she managed it carefully, the landlady wouldn't catch on that she was cooking with wood, not alcohol. With stumps of candles set around their portable hearth, they had enough light to see each other's faces as they ate and talked.

They were quiet together for hours on end in their one room. Or they talked, read, dreamed, played and prayed.

Their rapport was the opening through which Kafka was carried farther than he had ever been before into a living relationship with Yiddishkeit. After the Sabbath, Dora recited Havdalah, which separates the time of rest from the work week; Kafka swayed to the rhythm of the prayer. During the week, they sometimes attended lectures on the Talmud at the Academy for the Study of Judaism. Dora was interested in Halakhah, the ongoing never-to-be concluded debates of the sages, ancient and modern, regarding the Law. Kafka cared more for Aggada, the legends and stories with which the rabbis burrowed under the letter of the Law and discovered passages in which he found confirmation of a hidden force that went on acting in its own direction, at an immense distance from profane happiness. He listened in delight when one of the lecturers—to show the continuing influence of Midrash on contemporary writing—read Agnon's fable of the white goat, a she-goat that knew the way through a cave to a shortcut between Galicia and Safed, the town where the great mystics had lived and written their books. The sick old man, to whom the goat brought back milk from the Promised Land, wanted to know where she went when she disappeared, so his son tied a cord to the goat's tail and when he felt a pull on it he followed her through the cave to the other side of the world. He sent back a note to his father, which he folded in the goat's ear, so that when his father patted her head, as he always did, she would flick her ears and the note would fall out.

But this time the goat didn't flick her ears, the note didn't fall out, the father cursed the goat for leading his son astray and had her slaughtered.

As he and the butcher were skinning her, the note fell out, and he read to his horror that if he were to take up the cord and follow the goat, he would reach the Promised Land and rejoice with his son. The old man had to live out his days in exile.

From that time on, the mouth of the cave has been hidden.

Kafka entered the dream of the text as if it were his own. But he listened with ironic detachment when another lecturer explained that "the wind from the East" that blew open a path of escape for the Jews in Exodus was actually the result of a volcanic eruption, and by the time the lecture was done, nothing was left of the parting of the Red Sea but a concatenation of geological, geographical and meteorological facts.

*

In Berlin, Kafka tried—it was only the second time that he had tried—to write a story whose protagonist is identified as a Jew. A particular Jew, the living and breathing Jew trapped in the ghetto of the imaginary Jew, the one that the goyim accused of the blood libel. Who today remembers the Hilsner Affair? Yet it spread fear through the Jewish community of Prague at the turn of the twentieth century. Kafka was sixteen at the time. Then in 1911, Mendl Beilis was arrested for murdering a Christian boy and using his blood to bake matzah. Violence against Jews, the violence that Kafka had lived through during the days of December 1897—crowds roaming the city, smashing Jewish windows, breaking into synagogues, beating up anyone who looked like a Jew—the "December Storm" returned from the realm of forgetting where it was consigned to the past by believers in progress, flooding their memories, forcing them back into the cramped lives they thought they had left behind forever.

That was the year that Kafka entered the stream of collective Jewish experience through the Yiddish theater. He discovered in himself pockets of Jewishness that he did and did not want to dip into. When he was a boy on his way to school, he had run past the Altneu Synagogue whistling as loud as he could. The remains of the golem were said to be scattered in the dust of the attic whose high window looked down on him. His father dismissed the story as *narishkeit*, foolishness, but that didn't rid him of his fear and belief in the golem, the creature of brute strength that the Maharal, the Rabbi of Prague, had created to protect the Jews in times of danger. Years later, he tried to pour his boyhood experience into the story of how the Master of esoteric words breathed life into a lump of clay and created Joseph Golem in the likeness of a servant. Kafka had barely begun the story when he lost control of it. As the clay seemed to be acquiring a human form, the Rabbi of Prague became agitated, his hands started to shake, he thrust them so violently into the basin of water beside him, the water splashed up to the ceiling of the bare vault. The thing was already running amok—better to leave it a muddy stain, a miscarriage. Now, in Berlin, he wanted to return to the subject that had defeated him in the past. At the same moment, in New York, the Yiddish poet Leivick wrote his play, *The Golem*. "To me," Adrienne said, "this play suggests what flashed up in the imagination of Kafka's rabbi as he was giving form to his servant." In Leivick's play, the golem appears in public as a hewer of wood and a bearer of water. What the Yiddish poet adds to the legend is the ax that he has the golem carry with him everywhere as a disguise, a tool to crash through doors, and a weapon against enemies. The ax makes the golem as terrifying to the Jews as he is dangerous to the goyim; in the end the rabbi has to destroy his creation.

Kafka, master of the pitiless gaze, could do nothing until he viewed himself without alibis and made himself answerable for his failures. In examining his earlier effort to create something that could stand up to the fear induced by the blood libel, he grasped in an image what had previously eluded him: his interest lay not with the rabbi, but with the golem, the mute isolate creature that the rabbi endowed with the power of invisibility, so that the goyim would see his ax flying through air as if hurled by the unseen hand of the God of Vengeance, and the ax pursued them through winding streets, penetrated the subterranean chambers where they poured innocent blood into vials, and foiled their plot to plant incriminating evidence in the matzah factory. It was too late, Kafka told Dora, to insert his magical ax into the legend. He had used it in his story of the country doctor; it would lose its singular force if he were to repeat it; he had lost his chance of making the golem story his own. But the moment he gave up the golem, his interest shifted back to the rabbi, or rather the golem in the rabbi, who brings to consciousness, judges, and puts to death the brutal messianic inclination of his heart.

In Berlin, he was drawn back to the peculiar sensation that had passed through him twice a day when he passed under the golem's window as a boy. His whole body became so cold he felt no fire could ever warm him. No one was permitted in that attic; it was one of the holiest Jewish places in all of Europe, but it was only an attic, a *genizah*, a dusty place for concealing scraps of parchment with the holy tongue written on them. There was no one to watch over the Jews of Prague, no one to supervise what went on in these streets in the days and hours before a pogrom broke out. And yet something of the golem remained up there, in the attic of the Altneu Synagogue, and there was something in the coldness that swept over him twice a day when he passed under it, something that wouldn't exist unless he found the words to describe it. But he couldn't reach it by trying to bring the rabbi's clay messiah back to life. The thing that made writing a consuming search for redemption—its openness to what could not be known before meeting it as Moses met the burning bush, with no understanding of what he was seeing— would be foreclosed if he approached it in the traditional way, through the rabbi's story. To preserve the rabbi's search he had to forego the rabbi, much as he felt, in telling this to Dora, an atavistic tug, a nostalgia previously foreign to him. He still wanted something from the rabbi, something native to him, which he found in the story of the butchering of the she-goat: the daring of the holy imagination, the unpredictability and violence of the midrashic way. He wished to break into and enter a story that existed apart from him, a story in which the Jews lived their life and recognized their fate. What if he remained loyal to the midrashic way in the territory where it didn't belong, and started out from a text assigned to the Jews by History? What if he told the story of the trial of Mendl Beilis as though it were his own? And it was: all of Jewry had been put on trial with Beilis.

Just then Adrienne glanced at her watch. "Gotta go," she said. She was juggling many gigs. Work on her Kafka project was frequently interrupted. During these interruptions, new thoughts came to her and led her off in unanticipated directions, sometimes to the enrichment of the work, often to its detriment. In fits and starts, she accumulated promising images, insights, passages. Once, as she was rushing off to a rehearsal, at the moment of realizing that the piece she was reading to me would lead to interminable complications, she said, "I can't tell you how much time I waste trying to connect every last fragment to all the others. It's easy for me to taste Kafka's joy in destruction. I hate the demon that drives me to stop and tell you this when I'm already running late."

*

The next time we met, Adrienne didn't launch right in, as she usually did. She stood at the window, looking out at the yacht basin below us, and the river with its little pleasure crafts and gigantic barges. I was startled when, still facing away from me, she began to speak; something in her solemnity felt like a rebuke. Something familiar to me from before I was born—a spasm of uncontrollable anxiety. I began searching my mind for something I'd done that might have offended her.

"Promise me," she said, "that you won't breathe a word of what I'm about to tell you." I promised. "I haven't written any of this down, you understand." I understood. "I had the idea of volunteering at the Nagel Avenue Y because of all the refugees and survivors who go there. The director suggested that I teach a course on Kafka. After the first class, an elegant, trim Viennese refugee came up to me and told me that she had known Dora Diamont in London after the war, they became friends, and Dora confided in her. So Dita Hirsch and I began going out for coffee after the class, and I learned from her certain things that would probably have been lost if we hadn't met. Would you believe that she had me sign a letter of agreement stating that I would give her ten percent of my royalties on my book? Naturally, I agreed. Anyway, I'm looking for at least one other person who can corroborate the things she told me. Without written documentation, how can I prove that I've recovered one of Kafka's lost stories?

I'm hardly the first who's relied on interviews with Kafka's contemporaries. There's already enough evidence to show that traces of his art and life for which no papers exist survived the war in the collective memory of the Jewish people. How fitting that memory and word-of-mouth alone rescued the Beilis story from oblivion. Here's the seed of the story, which Dora told Dita and Dita told me. It was set in a Russian prison after the Jew's arrest. During his long months of imprisonment, the supervisor, as Kafka called him, reviewed his former life as the supervisor of a brick kiln and was tormented by the ritual murder that he had not committed."

Imprisonment, isolation, interrogation—the story began well, Adrienne told me. Kafka depicted the conditions under which the implausible became plausible, false memories proliferated as his captors woke him again and again and led him from his cell to a small black room where they went back over the charges against him. He knew perfectly well that he was innocent, but they would hear none of it. They offered to release him if he admitted his guilt and accepted an amnesty; he demanded to be put on trial. He could sooner forget that he was his mother's son than let them use him as living proof of the blood libel. Yet his days became confused, his sleep was interrupted by chain hearings, in the hands of his tormentors he realized that he was capable of murder, although he knew he hadn't done it. This knowledge meant nothing during the nights of interrogation, the days of obsession. His cell stank of his filth. Kafka lay in bed, coughing and writing; he had broken through to the vital place in himself where he normally suffered in silence, where his suffering made him identical to every other imprisoned, obstinate Jew; he gave voice to the shame induced by the charges against Beilis, against Hilsner, against himself—the shame induced by the unending assault on the image of the Jew.

As the story progressed, Kafka seemed to grow stronger. Dora dared to hope that he would recover as he had recovered in the past. He worked at the table, went out for walks with his notebook, ready to take down any phrase or impression that offered itself; he returned tired but refreshed. Dora was elated by this turn of events. So she was all the more devastated when three days went by without his writing anything. On the fourth day, he was back in bed, coughing and shivering under two blankets and a quilt.

*

After the funeral, at the shiva, Brod asked Dora if he could speak with her in Franz's bedroom. It was exactly as Kafka had left it, except for the black cloth draped over the mirror. Brod came right to the point. He asked Dora to hand over to him all his friend's manuscripts and letters. She said it couldn't be done. He stared at her in disbelief. She had no choice, he said, he was the executor of Kafka's literary estate. She stiffened, and said quietly that he had ordered her to burn his outlines and notes, and an unfinished story about Mendl Beilis. As a result of this, she said, their secret stove could no longer be kept hidden, and they were forced to move. It was the loss to world literature, rather than their precarious domestic arrangements, that horrified Brod. He felt nauseous and suddenly sleepy; he yawned and, sucking in air, suppressed the roar out of the words he uttered, "You betrayed him." He grabbed the edge of Kafka's desk to support himself and to restrain the impulse that made his right hand tremble violently. "No," she said coolly, "it's you who betray him—you want to save every scrap of paper he wanted to burn, you refuse to carry out the sentence he pronounced over his unfinished work." "Shame on you," Brod hissed. He pulled himself up to his full height and dropped his voice into the barrel-chested basso that commanded impressive speaking fees from Jewish audiences all over Europe. He proceeded to lecture her: his voice filled the room, the floor under his feet ceased quivering. With his right index finger, he pointed to Kafka's chair and said, "An author is the last person on earth you can look to for an objective judgment about his work. No writer was more unmerciful than Franz. He was quick to see his defects. He would write a sentence and immediately cross it out. A misplaced comma, a sentence with too much or too little in it—it stopped him cold. He needed always to be writing at the top of his bent. I've never said this aloud before, Dora—he was a fanatic, and though I believe that the golden mean makes life good for most of us, I think that his fanaticism was legitimate. His work made the leap beyond realism into another way of writing—he didn't emphasize what writing has in common with living, but what makes writing different. In writing, the pressure to keep things intelligible—the pressure that makes it possible for us to bear ourselves and live in the world—gets in the way. Automatic responses, familiar terms like the golden mean, the ideas and metaphors we live by slip in and take over. What comes out is the expectable thing, it's what we already know, what we repeat every day of our lives, what keeps a lid on the things we glimpse as fantasies but cannot think or say to anyone, including ourselves—all this so-called living stuff must be purged. What's left is writing, but if you take this too far, nothing is left."

"You think you know, but you don't," she said.

Brod was shocked at her presumption, this little woman from an ignorant background—he had never been so insulted by a woman.

She said with quiet authority, "That wasn't why he

burned the Beilis story with his own hands."

Because she knew: it was too frank a confession of the shame that Western Jews hated to admit to themselves, let alone anyone else. He felt in her a power that he would not be able to shame into submission. What did she know that he didn't? What was she keeping from him? If he asked her to explain, he would be taking the one-down position, but he needed to know. Hadn't he often put his ego aside in the service of his friend? Yes, he needed to act with humility as befit the guardian of the Kafka Estate. In a respectful voice, he asked Dora to tell him what she knew.

"He had his own reasons for burning his notebooks," she said. "But what triggered it just then was that we'd run out of money. There was a sudden frost and I couldn't scavenge any fuel. Franz was running a high fever, he couldn't stand seeing my lips and fingers turn blue. He ordered me to burn his manuscripts to heat the room."

Brod, wavering between skepticism and astonishment, asked for more detail. "After returning from a foraging expedition," Dora said, "I found him propped up against the wall, his head was thrown forward in uncontrollable spasms of coughing, his coughing had the ghastly sound of suffocation, his whole body fought for air, billows of black smoke poured from the wood-burning stove. Gasping for breath, Kafka said, 'I've only succeeded—Shush, don't speak'—but he went on— 'in burning the Beilis…. Dora, you're going to have to finish the job.'"

His blue valise lay open beside him. Only then did she take in what she had seen when she walked into the room. He was unpacking his notebooks, tearing the pages out of them, and feeding them to the fire.

Quickly, she scooped him up, she told Brod, and

carried him to bed. During the trip across the room, he let his head fall against her breast, closed his eyes and fell asleep. She remembered what he had said shortly after they met. He had warned her to leave him at once. "I worry what will become of you if you tie your fate—and your body—to mine." In her arms, this body—it now weighed less than a hundred pounds—felt skeletal. It hurt her to carry its unyielding weight, which cut into her flesh as if it were patched together out of two by fours, a poorly made manikin. When she lowered him into bed, his eyes snapped open, he looked up at her in alarm. She caressed his cheek and he dropped back to sleep.

She opened the window—only a few inches, it was one of those November days that carried more than a threat of December—to allow the room to clear of smoke. Her ministrations gave the fire the respite it needed to revive, it burst into flames, sounding like the happy uproar of a well-tended family hearth.

51. KAFKA'S COMMAS

In the new room, also unheated, he wrote "The
Burrow." Under three layers of clothing and a blanket,
he resumed the practice of his craft, sounding out his
sentences in his mind's ear, to test them, to make sure he
got their tempo just right, before swooping down on them
and resuming his siege against normative German syntax,
regulated by punctuation that stifled the mimetic rhythm
of his prose, now terse, now sidewinding, now panting
and bursting, now prowling around, shifting without
transition, an unrelenting momentum. It was the cadence
of his sentences that first earned him Brod's admiration and
love, but Brod had never understood his early struggle with
punctuation. His hesitation, his sense of inadequacy, had to
do with the hold that the conventions of grammar still had
over him. Yet by the time he had written "The Wish to Be a
Red Indian," he had already discovered what swiftness and
force could be gained by omitting the period. "In general,"
he noted in his diary, "the spoken sentence begins in a large
capital letter with the speaker, bends out on its course as far
as it can toward the listeners and with the period returns
to the speaker. If the period is omitted, then the sentence
is no longer constrained and blows its entire breath at the
listener." In that little one-sentence story, he had released the
full blast of his rushing spirit, immediately removing from
the realm of the eye what he heaped up, phrase by phrase, in
the field of the breath. Now, as in the past, it returned of its
own accord, and it almost never failed to please and surprise
him, to fire him up for the work ahead. "If one were only an

Indian, instantly alert, and on a racing horse, leaning against the wind, quivering over the quivering ground, until one shed one's spurs, for no spurs were needed, threw away the reins, for no reins were needed, and hardly saw the land before him was smoothly shorn heath when the horse's neck and head would already be gone." Writing as speech and speech as song, reviving pleasure and the wish to fade away in a racing image! The triumph achieved by that horse and rider had been won by daring to let go of any punctuation, except commas, within that endless sentence.

Now quiet, steadied, ready to go back to the hard labor of finishing "The Burrow." He had written it spontaneously—it had written itself—until it came to an abrupt halt. While he waited for the voice speaking to him in the dark to come again, he decided to kill time productively, and perhaps by yielding all the initiative to the voice, spur it to go on with his story; he decided to go back over it, sentence by sentence, to listen to what he had written, and punctuate it accordingly.

A voice in the dark, a badger or mole making the rounds of the passages of his burrow—he kept coming up against unforeseen problems; the techniques he had mastered when young no longer sufficed. Kafka saw he was in the same bind as his creature; he saw that the commas of the past no longer worked.

COMMAS INTO SEMI-COLONS, LABYRINTHIAN SENTENCES

In "The Burrow," the commas of the past no longer worked. The speaker of the story, the vulnerable creature in his labyrinth, breathed in anxiety, and exhaled its destructive effects. He was the nameless maker of his world, the hammering head that designed and constructed the labyrinth—the maze of passages around the exit that became a model and a metaphor for the entire burrow—but the manifold proliferating possibilities that he envisioned underwent abrupt changes, under the sway of his anxious thoughts; safe passages turned into threatening ones, sites of terrifying presentiments, unceasing reversals; success collapsed into failure, tranquility into fear, what was hidden was exposed to danger; he could tell by "the almost inaudible whistling noise that wakened [him]" out of a light sleep. Once he heard it, it never ceased harassing him; "it goes on always on the same thin note with regular pauses, now a sort of whistling, but again like a kind of piping." Here, one sentence couldn't predict the length and course of another. The secret of the sentences of "The Burrow"—without warning, the palpable but unstated meaning of their rhythm flips from a creative to a destructive force; as a creative force, it must be released, allowed to flow on; as a destructive force, it had to be stopped; or it had to be prevented from attaining its end as long as possible.

He picked out a passage near the beginning of the story and tinkered with it, in the hope that it could provide him with a template for punctuating the entire work, even though he knew that every attempt he had made in the past to solve this problem in a systematic way had failed. Nonetheless, as soon as he isolated the technical issues that preoccupied him, he felt sharp, powerful, engaged, and went through the passage, getting rid of its difficulties. He then read it to Dora, commenting on the attack—the shifting methods of attack—of the punctuation against the words. In the voice of the threatened creature, he said: "I must have the confident knowledge that somewhere there is an exit easy to reach and quite free, where I have to do nothing to get out, so that I might never—Heaven shield us—suddenly feel the teeth of the pursuer in my flank while I am desperately burrowing away, even if it is at loose easy soil."

A pause, then in his own soft, low and incisive voice: "Long-breath sentence, the sentence of commas, imitating the confident knowledge, but, stricken suddenly by dread of the end, it rushes through the winding, obstructed passageway to the exit."

The creature continued: "And it is not only by external enemies that I am threatened. There are also enemies in the bowels of the earth. I have never seen them, but legends tell of them and I firmly believe in them."

Kafka commented: "Reign of the declarative, the statement of objective conditions, and the object of legends. Raising and thwarting consciousness of the contradiction between the objective and the legendary, the sentence nails its subject to its conclusion with a period."

The creature elaborated: "They are creatures of the inner earth; not even legend can describe them. Their very victims can scarcely have seen them; they come, you hear the scratching of their claws under you in the ground, which is their element, and already you are lost. Here it is of no avail to console yourself with the thought that you are in our own house; far rather you are in theirs. Not even my exit could save me from them; indeed, in all probability it would not save me in any case, but rather betray me; yet it is a hope, and I cannot live without hope. Apart from the main exit I am also connected with the outer world by quite narrow, tolerably safe passages which provide me with good fresh air to breathe."

Kafka cut in: "Enter the semi-colon, agent of the period, a divided and dividing thing, half-period, half-comma, undoing whatever preceded it; multiplying rapidly, sinking its claws into the simple sentence and rendering it null and void;

interrupting the smooth and steady progression of thought to mark the impasse it cannot escape from, to place doubt side-by-side with belief—unsustainable belief—intolerable doubt, making a world where there is no sure path to being saved."

To be admitted into the inner sanctum of his art—Dora felt that everything he wrote in their room was addressed to her.

She had been bored and frustrated by this latest story when he first read excerpts of it to her; now she followed it with plea-sure. It was about his life before he met her, she thought. One thing hadn't changed: he needed to make every sentence per-fect, and the exertion of it could lead to a state of exhaustion in which everything looked bad to him, but he went on trying to make progress anyway, increasingly desperate, fearful that in the end he would have to abandon it.

She encouraged him to go on. He finished a few more pages, read them to her, and received back the hush of her complete attention saturated by the *ts*-sound that hasidim make in the face of something astonishing, wonderful, praise-worthy. It was about her life too, she thought, and the life of every Jew, the vague threat they all felt, their fear of the goyim, the private ghetto they each carried on their backs after leaving the visible ghetto. He read to her, confident in the knowledge that what he had written was built to last.

In "The Burrow," commas break up the continu-ity and connection between phrase and phrase; semi-colons crop up in many passages, stop little sentences from becom-ing terminal, extend them by contradicting them, until the breakdown of the sense of the sentence that they implement runs up against the check of the period. "All that can be seen from outside is a big hole; that, however, leads nowhere; if you take a few steps you strike against natural firm rock." Here, the breath moves through obstacles of many kinds—reversals of meaning; paranoid logic; intended and unintended deceptions; unformulated gaps; barriers marked by semi-colons—which render audible the resistance, the countermovement against reaching the end of the sentence. Here, the task of the comma is not to rush things along toward their goal, but to defer their arrival, to draw out the race against an almost inaudible force that threatens to destroy the speaker. Here, the comma needs to be reinforced, needs a period placed on top of it, to give it weight, pin it down, convert it into a semi-colon.

He went back to revising the story.

Dora sat in the enormous silence of the room against which Kafka's wheezing and coughing sounded all the more loud. But he was absorbed in his work; he seemed unaware of the noises that came out of him. And he was so at ease with her that he was free to lose himself in thought as she watched him dot commas, change semi-colons to periods, and cut passages when he couldn't save them by less drastic means.

Permanent Tasks of the Comma

As he reviews the story, he becomes aware of what he didn't know while writing it; only in retrospect can he parse the process through which he discovered how it would unfold. The punctuation in all its variability carries on the task that the comma pioneered in his first book. Now as always, the task of the comma is to score the text as spoken speech, to raise it from the page onto the breath, so that he might become more aware of it; and simultaneously, it is a technique for making sentences mimic their shifting subjects of enunciation, in this case, the passages of the burrow going off in unexpected directions, the movement of the speaker's

thought negating itself and descending ever deeper into a
state of vigilance and terror, and the sound of the speaker's
labored breathing, which he delusively takes as the noise of a
great beast, a beast that bores with its teeth and claws toward
him through the burrow walls. And there is something else
in these labyrinthian sentences; even as they represent the
speaker's environment, the dynamics of his inner world, and
the twists and turns of his actions, they reflexively describe
their own construction and movement. "When I stand in the
Castle Keep surrounded by my piled-up stores, surveying the
ten passages which begin here, raised and sunken passages,
vertical and rounded passages, wide and narrow passages,
as the general plan dictates, and all alike still and empty,
ready by their various routes to conduct me to all the other
rooms, which are also still and empty—then all thought of
mere safety is far from my mind, then I know that here is my
castle...." The Kafkan sentence, taking its origin from his own
tubercular breathing and making itself its own subject in its
flight from attachment to the world, the self and its acts—it
coils round and round as though to enclose a space without
beginning or end, but the space is empty, the correspondences
through which life becomes art and eternal are something
that we in our lack supply, so how can the sentence ever be
finished when it was invented to trap us in our own fear of
the unknown, in our particular obsession with something or
someone who might be a way out of it?

Toward the Last Gasp, Commas in the Gap

At Zurau, convalescing after his cough and fever were
diagnosed as tuberculosis, he had written aphorisms about
"the last things." He had speculated about the gap between
being and consciousness; and in his reflections on hope and

the true way, he had written that there is "a state of being that craves the last breath, craves suffocation." This laid the groundwork for "The Burrow," an elaborate structure devised to keep that craving from coming to consciousness. Yet it is that very state of being, the creaturely suffering and depletion in which the wish to die arises, toward which the swollen sentences of "The Burrow," overtaxing and obstructing the finite flow of breath, aim.

In This Series of Shifting Identities

Glimpses of the end that the speaking animal desires and wards off appear in four crucial passages, but each of these passages is marked by the false consciousness of the speaker. Each time he foresees his death, he is somebody else; he hides the pain of his existence and his terror of non-existence by shifting his identity and assuming an ideological position that allows him briefly to deny his basic state, that of persecutory anxiety. The creature doesn't really know who or what he is, he doesn't know that he doesn't know this, nor does he know that he is continually trying out different subject positions in a futile effort to come to terms with his death.

In the first of these passages, he is the artist/intellectual who built "the beautifully vaulted chamber" of his central storehouse, the Castle Keep, out of the poor materials that he was given to work with—loose and sandy soil that he had pounded and hammered into a firm state to serve as a wall. "But for such tasks the only tool that I possess is my forehead. So I had to run with my forehead thousands and thousands of times, for whole days and nights, against the soil, and I was glad when the blood came, because that was proof the walls were beginning to harden; and in that way, as everybody must admit, I richly paid for my Castle Keep." A ironic portrait of the drivenness and anguish of the late romantic artist. As in dreamwork, the Kafkan creature turns a familiar expression— to bang one's head against the wall—into a strange image in which unspoken and mutually antagonistic meanings are condensed. The creature's aggression against himself is disguised from himself under his overriding sense of futility, which is acted out but denied verbal expression under the regime of his self-sacrificing devotion to his creative labor.

In the second of these quickly disappearing depictions of the creature in the grip of the death drive, the speaker appears to be the weary pilgrim, yearning to leave the woods, the world of toil and danger where he hunts and is hunted. "I am not permanently doomed to this free life, because I know that my term is measured, that I do not have to hunt here forever, and that, whenever I am weary of this life and wish to leave it, Someone, whose invitation I shall not be able to withstand, will, so to speak, summon me to him. And so I can pass the time here quite without care and in complete enjoyment, or rather I could, and yet I cannot. My burrow takes up too much of my thoughts."

In the third variation of this theme, the speaker turns up as the householder, the citizen willing to die to defend his home and homeland, the bourgeois whose peacefulness is secured under the watchwords of "blood and soil." After a detailed survey of the maze of ten passages that guard his castle, the householder asserts that they have a higher purpose than mere safety: "then I know that here is my castle, which I have wrested from the refractory soil with tooth and claw, with pounding and hammering blows, my castle which can never belong to anyone else, and is so essentially mine that I can calmly accept in it my enemy's mortal stroke at the final hour, because my blood will ebb away here on my own soil and will not be lost. And what but that is the meaning of the blissful hours I pass, now peacefully slumbering, now happily keeping watch, in these passages, these passages which suit me so well, where one can stretch oneself out in comfort, roll about in childish delight, lie and dream, or sink into blissful sleep."

By dramatizing the speaker's diffuse identity, his lack of identity with himself as he moves through shallow but intense subject positions—as the artist/intellectual creature, the religious creature, and the nationalistic bourgeois creature—Kafka makes the gap between his being and his consciousness explicit. Throughout these changes, the creature remains animated by countercurrents of fear and desire that elude his determined efforts to uncover the source of his anxiety. Here, glimpses of the aim of the creature's life—which is death, the Kafkan thanatos—are seen in reverse through the mirror of ideologies that embrace what the creature fears, ascribe a redemptive meaning to the senseless pain that gradually drains the creature of his will to live, and infuse that meaning with lofty feelings: the artist's sense of accomplishment, even of greatness, as he contemplates the beauty of his work; the pilgrim's deliverance from the tribulations of this world and his union with a higher power; the bourgeois householder's sense of comfort, and beyond that, of bliss and immortality, attained through incorporating himself into something lasting and great, his homeland. All this elevated thought and feeling serve to lead the reader away from the gap that is not to be found in the distorting glass of the speaker's hopes and beliefs, yet its trace is evident throughout the text, and searching for the truth about it becomes the speaker's main project.

In the fourth and final repetition in this series of shifting identities, the speaker appears to have abandoned his quest for the fulfillment of his wish for more life and takes up the stance of the empiricist truth seeker, the scientific investigator obsessed with the whistling noise that awakens him from a light sleep in his favorite room. He undertakes a systematic investigation of his burrow, to verify his conviction that the noise is being caused by little creatures burrowing a channel in his walls, which traps the air, and these "stoppages of the current of air" produce the whistling in the walls. In his meticulous search, it is "the technical problem that most attracts [him]." He makes his way through the burrow, passage by passage, room by room, "on fire to discover whether my conclusion is valid. And with good reason, for as long as that is not established I cannot feel safe." No matter where he turns or what he tries, he can't locate the source of the noise that troubles him; as the area of the unknown extends to every nook and cranny of his refuge, the danger becomes more alarming and by the time the story comes to an abrupt halt, unfinished, the many little creatures have been reconfigured in the speaker's fantasy as a great beast coming through the walls to tear him apart.

Now, in the area of his terrifying uncertainty, he is compelled to face the fact that he has reached an impasse: "I can find nothing, no matter how hard I search, or it may be that I find too much. This had to happen just in my favorite room, I think to myself, and I walk a fair good distance away from it, almost half-way along the passage leading to the next room; but I do this merely as a joke, pretending to myself that my favorite room is not alone to blame, but that there are disturbances elsewhere as well, and with a smile on my face I begin to listen; but soon I stop smiling, because, right enough, the same whistling meets me here too. It is really nothing to worry about; sometimes I think that nobody but myself would hear it; it is true, I hear it now more and more distinctly, for my ear has grown keener through practice; though in reality it is exactly the same noise wherever I may hear it, as I have convinced myself by comparing my impressions. Nor is it growing louder; I recognize this when I listen in the middle of the passage instead of pressing my ear against the wall. Then it is only by straining my ears, indeed by lowering my head as well, that I can more guess at than hear the merest trace of a noise now and then. But it is this very uniformity of the noise everywhere that disturbs me most, for it cannot be made to agree with my original assumption. Had I rightly divined the cause of the noise, then it must have issued with greatest force from some given place, which it would be my task to discover. And after that grown fainter and fainter. But if my hypothesis does not meet the case, what can the explanation be?"

Here, Kafka directly poses the question, and offers all the information needed to answer it, which invites the reader to make the leap in thought that would uncover the gap in which the creature struggles to make sense of his situation. His burrow is the paradoxical place of refuge where he hears the echo of his own breathing as the augury of his last breath. The technical problem for Kafka, in his effort to finish off this passage, is to mark the stoppages of the air so that, as the reader breathes life into the words, she will feel what the creature feels. A terrified creature of flesh and blood scrambling for reassurance! How far from the days when he wished to be an Indian leaning against the wind into which he disappears! And yet how close—he is back in the medium of racing thoughts, only now no ecstasy of image-making conceals his wish to die. The writing of the gap in "The Burrow" is charged with a feeling of anxiety that the semi-colons are there to contain, but cannot, as, one by one, the speaker's rationalizations break down, and the craving for the last breath comes up against the craving for more breath; the creature strains to listen and lowers his head, a gesture of old determination and new submission; his denial gives way to heightened vigilance, and the phrasing takes its pace from the mounting anxiety that floods his words, his furious search for the truth continues, but only commas, nothing but commas in the gap between phrase and phrase—they won't stop the creature's panic from forcing his powers of reasoning from conceding defeat.

Not for long. He transforms the absence of the little creatures into the presence of the great beast, and resumes his technical investigations, digging trenches here and there and stopping at certain intervals to listen. The story breaks off where he imagines that if his murderous disappearing opponent had heard him, he "must have noticed some sign of it, the beast must at least have stopped its work every now and then to listen. But all remained unchanged."

IN THE BRIEF INTERVALS BETWEEN THEIR STRUGGLES

In the sanatorium at Kierling, he sat up all night correcting galleys of "The Hunger Artist." Dora sat with him, wide awake despite exhaustion; she felt her vigilance sustain his, flow into his, add onto his, giving him the strength to complete his last book. Toward dawn, he put the galleys aside, lay down beside her, and talked about commas. 'Each is a little pick-ax, a blow against the syntax of strength, against the muteness of language, to make the sentence open its mouth, take a deep breath, cry out, then again the comma is a trial of strength, a blow struck at the sentence to silence it, if the sentence proves stronger than the attempt to destroy it, it is left, punctured, with wounds on its side, concessive or disjunctive clauses punctuated lightly, with commas, the sentence goes on breathing, the breath rises and falls through all of it, carrying the voice, the full voice, the singing voice through each interval, each blow."

Again, as in Berlin, Dora felt him admitting her into his holy of holies, the place he kept hidden even from Brod, his workshop, where he practiced his craft. This being together, this breathing together inside his sentences with him—it was as intimate as going to bed with him, and even more intimate. The one absolute in her life now was anticipating his every need, and meeting it insofar as it was possible.

In the afternoon, he began proofreading the mouse fable, his last story. He told Dora that it was painful to have to go into it again, to have to experience it all again. It released as much feeling in him now as when he first wrote it. "Listen," he said, and he read her the following passage: "Here in the brief intervals between their struggles our people dream, it is as if the limbs of each were loosened, as if the harried individual once in a while could relax and stretch himself at ease in the great, warm bed of the community. And into these dreams Josephine's piping drops note by note; she calls it pearl-like, we call it staccato; but at any rate here it is in its right place, as nowhere else, finding the moment wait for it as music scarcely ever does. Something of our poor brief childhood is in it, something of lost happiness that can never be found again, but also something of active daily life, of its small gaieties, unaccountable and yet springing up and not to be obliterated. And indeed this is all expressed not in full round tones but softly, in whispers, confidentially, sometimes a little hoarsely. Of course it is a kind of piping. Why not? Piping is our people's daily speech, only many a one pipes his whole life long and does not know it, where here piping is set free from the fetters of daily life and it sets us free too for a little while. We certainly should not want to do without these performances."

He looked directly at her and said something about lost happiness that could never be found again. And then to have gone on and written those sentences…. It was as though he, too, was astonished at their music. But this little performance had tired him out. He tired quickly, and in his weariness doubts sprang up, doubts collected themselves around his commas, these miniscule gap-markers, markers of silence and breath, these holes in speech, these drains; he lacked the conviction to certify his original choices or chop into the sentence again and, by interrupting it at another point, create the interval that gave the last word its echo, undermining it as the final word by asserting the gap in which it awaited the next one. He felt each comma stuck in his throat. His doctor's diagnosis was that the tuberculosis had spread to his larynx. He could barely swallow, he was starving to death. A little water, sipped through a straw, burned his vocal cords so badly, he lay drowning in curses he couldn't spit out.

Toward evening, unable to bear the sight of his wounded sentences, his eyes helped out, they clouded over, but his everlasting clear-sightedness returned. He had Dora bundle him up in two blankets and a comforter, he went back to work. In his weariness he was tempted to end all commas, dislodge them from every sentence, do something utterly new, a stream of words without punctuation, but he stayed his hand, knowing that his impulse to clean up the mess on the page was itself impure.

Let there be a rest from this rage for purity. He shut his eyes, slept, dreamed a little. He was back in the room in Berlin with mice squeaking in the walls as they had in his room in his parents' house.

Dora saw him fall forward, stop breathing, she thought he had had a stroke. She ran screaming into the corridor. Kafka was spared this scene. He had fainted after a bout of coughing. The doctor gave him a shot. He slept soundly. In the morning, propped up in bed again, he was back at the galleys, picking away at his questionable commas, one by one, purging them or letting them pass.

A HIDDEN HISTORY

It was hardly a surprise to Brod—a believer in hope and ultimate redemption—that Kafka, after a lifetime of wretched relations with women, should have been sent a ministering angel to watch over him during his final days on earth. Despite his rage at Dora for having burned Kafka's manuscripts, he realized that a devoted girl like herself could have done nothing else but obey the man's instructions; and it was not without a certain sense of his own magnanimity that he got past his outrage to recognize, and be grateful for, her remarkable care for his dying friend.

And yet it wasn't true; Dora had lied to him. She believed that Kafka's papers were rightly hers, that his soul resided there more than anywhere else and that he intended her to possess them after he died; and she knew for certain that he didn't want them published, as Brod would have done. Yet it was most likely that they were burned after all, unless, by some miracle, they survived among millions of unsorted documents in warehouses that held the Nazi archives. In March, 1933, two months after Hitler came to power, her husband Ludwig Lask—an enemy of the state—fled to Moscow. She stayed behind to clear out of their apartment what she could pack into two suitcases. Rummaging through their rooms, she packed only essentials—a change of underwear, a toothbrush, soap, and the like. She didn't want to leave without a keepsake, but there were too many notebooks and letters, and no time to go through them, so she left them where they lay, in her bureau. The Gestapo seized every last scrap of paper with writing on it when they raided the apartment.

And yet she did manage to save a hidden letter of his, the most precious letter she could have found. She pulled down his copy of Casanova's memoirs from the place on her shelf reserved for his books—a lucky grab! He had taken it with him wherever he went, part of his small indispensable library. Brod thought that there was nothing behind his breathtaking and unprecedented prose but his own genius. How shocked he would have been to find out that Kafka had stolen Casanova's escape from prison as the source of many passages in *The Trial*. How carefully he had disguised his literary thefts, burning all his preparatory notes and keeping his near-verbatim quotations of Casanova and other writers that he loved hidden from his closest friend. The book dropped out of her trembling hand, and out of it fell a note in Kafka's light, fluid handwriting, a last letter intended for her and delivered by chance. She slipped it back between the pages of the book and took it out to read when she was on the train heading east to join her husband.

52. Story of the Woodcutter

       Over the course of many years, Adrienne Gottbaum pursued Kafka the Jewish storyteller in the only way that she could gain access to the Kafka she pursued—through the testimony of people who knew people who had known him. She did not neglect documentary sources; but these, apart from the sketch of the golem story that Kafka improvised and abandoned in his diary of 1916, led to an impasse. One of his biographers mentions a story about Mendl Beilis, the Jew who was accused of the blood libel in the same year (1911) that Kafka imaginatively entered the communal life of the Jews through the Yiddish theater, but that story was lost—until Adrienne found and interviewed Dita Hirsch, who heard it from Kafka's beloved Dora. After that, Adrienne was more than ever consumed by her project; she extended the time allotted for research, deferred trying to complete her work. As the major method of excavating Kafka's life and work, oral history was deemed unreliable and inefficient by scholarly investigators, so she largely had the field to herself. When she sent an article on the Beilis story to a prestigious journal, the peer reviewers ripped it to shreds, saying that while her reconstruction of the story was plausible, there was too little evidence to support her claims. Funding for her work dried up, but that didn't stop her. Through a combination of luck and persistence that sometimes bestows a retrospective appearance of reason and inevitability on an unlikely project, she discovered a third story that was openly Jewish in character.

       She heard it from an elderly survivor named Felix Feinblatt, a retired typewriter repairman who had been an aspiring actor in Poland. Adrienne had volunteered to conduct a reminiscence group in the Bialystoker Home on East Broadway. Six people had shown up, among them Felix. Initially, their memories were thin and fragmentary, or confined to set pieces worn smooth of living moments by repeated retelling. So Adrienne began each session with a topic that took them by surprise, that invoked specific memories and gave them a fixed point around which to cohere. She had them present a museum of first things, first times, a personal genesis story, using photos, drawings, mementos, anecdotes, interior monologues, dialogues. Or she had them walk in imagination through their childhood home, recollecting what they saw and felt there. Since they were all preoccupied with forgetting, she began one session by suggesting that they talk about forgetting. Felix, silent until then, said, "It's not only a bad thing, forgetting. It can be a blessing and an art."

He went into the center of the circle of folding chairs—more than half of them empty; nonetheless, it couldn't hurt to be prepared for an overflow crowd—in which the old people sat, and slowly rotated his body 360 degrees with his cupped hands extended to each of them in turn, begging for the attention that his formal gesture commanded from the group. At that moment, Adrienne stopped having to force herself to look at him. He was gaunt, with bulging eyes half-hidden under a brown fedora that he never took off. He kept flicking his tongue through his lips and pulling it back as though swallowing it.

"No one who wasn't there," he began, and stopped, making loud grating noises to clear his throat. "Sorry, first words of the day, windpipe's rusty. I'm saying no one can know what it was like.... Even if you were there... what you knew was only a tiny piece of it... and even that was far... [again, grating noises]... from the truth, because we didn't want to know...."

He paused, looked down, drew a deep breath; it was as if he had gone and returned as another person, who smiled, and took his time, or rushed, as he pleased, because he had become master of the stage on which the lost world was about to be unveiled again.

"In the ghetto," he said, "people spent as much time trying to find an hour of forgetfulness as they did on the black market, trading their last possessions for food. The ghetto offered a diverse menu of forgetting. In music, everything from string quartets to chamber orchestras. Lectures on every subject under the sun. Black humor galore in the streets, in work details, in bunkers. Of course, underground yeshivas flourished. And then there was the theater, forgetfulness of choice for me. I especially enjoyed the one-man shows of Jacques Löwy. The old Warsavians knew him as Yitzkhok Leyvi, but at some point in his travels he changed his name to Jacques Löwy, and made himself over into an unforgettable character, the better to help us forget where we were. On stage and off, he dressed like a dandy—a monocle in his left eye, a high stiff collar, formal pumps, and a derby. It took high spirits and a lot of playacting to keep up this role. Asthma and a life spent trying to extract recognition from Western audiences for Yiddish theater and his own place in it had left him with no hope for himself. Add to this the certainty that when they started liquidating the ghetto, he would be among the first to be taken, and you have a despair that would have been the end of me, as it was for so many. Not Jacques. He swaggered down the street with his silver-handled cane, he performed in basement cafés, he bragged about his friendship with Kafka, his false teeth clacked in his mouth when he recited poems by Shimon Frug or Yehuda HaLevi. Everything about him was artificial and exaggerated, anywhere else he would have been laughed at, as a fool and an impostor, but he was what we needed.

"He performed a type of one-man show that was popular in the era when the majority of the world's Jews lived their lives in Yiddish, a variety show that fused the declamatory style of the music hall with an anthology of familiar poems. But the featured piece of his repertoire—a storytelling performance that he put on at least once a week—was his rendition of a piece by Franz Kafka called 'Story of the Woodcutter.' He said that, in 1924, when his friend was dying in Berlin, he had visited him and asked for something by which he could remember him to the world—a story, even the briefest of stories, that he could take on the road and perform in theaters. On the spot, Kafka improvised a poetic tale, which, Löwy was proud to say, was a tribute to a parable that he, Jacques Löwy, had invented for his friend many years earlier in Prague. Kafka did him the honor of stealing a motif that he (Jacques Löwy) had taken from the stories of wonder-rabbis that he had heard as a child and that had entered modern Yiddish literature through a tale by I. L. Peretz— 'If Not Higher' —that had passed into the folklore out of which it arose. Jacques Löwy translated Kafka's story into Yiddish, introduced it by retelling the Peretz story, and, after seeing it flop in Western Europe, he found an audience for it in the Warsaw ghetto. When rumors went around that the Nazis had ordered the *Judenrat* to hand over 5000 Jews for transport to the East, Jacques came to me and said, 'Felix, Felix, in three days I don't expect to be here, so you will have to learn the Kafka piece and perform it. When you do, tell the story of how I came by it and handed it over to you.'

"In the ghetto, there were those who never tired of hearing it. They came to the makeshift theaters where I performed it to lose themselves in the story of Kafka's rabbi, a believer in hope, but the only kind of hope that seemed credible to them, because it barely amounted to a belief—in fact, it seemed absurd—and yet was taken as the basis for action. And they came because it spurred debates, and these debates kept us warm on freezing nights. This was an audience schooled in verbal battle—worker-intellectuals, people interested in the arts, journalists, professors, fugitives from the yeshivas. A few had read Kafka in the German. One of them, Moshe Shtarkman, a reviewer for *The Forward* in New York, doubted whether the piece about the woodcutter-rabbi had been written by Kafka, although it was in the Kafka vein of placing nostalgia for the messianic kingdom side by side with the impossibility of reaching it. Shtarkman thought it was likely that my friend and mentor Jacques Löwy had mimicked the Kafka thing to promote himself, but he didn't condemn him; on the contrary, he admired the comic actor's inventiveness, his will to go on, and if he created the illusion that he was bringing us into the world of one of the great Jewish storytellers, a Jew who wrote German better than the Germans, and made it bow down to Yiddish ironies and inflections, isn't that why we came to the theater?"

*

Adrienne arranged for Felix to perform "Story of the Woodcutter" in the auditorium of the Bialystoker Home. The event, held on a Sunday in April, was open to the residents of the nursing home, their families, and the remnant of the Yiddish-speaking world that still lived on the Lower East Side. "A pitiful turnout," she told me, "but Felix launched into his performance with immense verve. He imagined that Jacques

216

Löwy and Kafka were sitting in the front row." As she told me these things, she pulled a small black cassette player from the large bag of papers and books that she always carried, set it on my desk, and with a flourish of her right hand, she pressed *play*. A reedy voice issued from the black box, straining to make itself heard.

"Imagine," the voice said, "that you arrive at the town of Nemirov on the day before Yom Kippur. The night of penitential prayers is coming on, it's too late for you to reach the next town, so you start looking for a place to spend the night. Nowhere to be found. The *rebbe's* hasidim have come from near and far to be with him on the holiday. Everywhere you go, you are told that on the night of Selichot, the *rebbe* of Nemirov ascends to Heaven.

"A likely story. A familiar story. Do you doubt it? So did a certain traveler from the north, a cold-blooded man, a Litvak. A Litvak is scientific. He wants to see with his own eyes where the *rebbe* goes when he disappears from the midst of his community. So he does the scientific thing: hides under the *rebbe's* bed, to gather evidence.

"First thing he sees is the bundle of peasant's clothes appearing out of a closet: linen trousers, high boots, thick coat, big felt hat, a wide leather belt studded with brass nails. The *rebbe* quickly changes into this outfit; in the darkened room he could pass for a woodcutter. The end of a heavy rope dangles from his coat pocket.

"Next thing the Litvak sees is the ax. The *rebbe* pulls it out of the closet and whispers something to it in Polish. The Litvak shudders. He watches the *rebbe* put the ax in his belt and slip out before the midnight call to prayer.

"Then what? He follows, he watches. The *rebbe* enters the dark wood at the edge of town, he feels himself become holy through and through. He gathers some fallen branches which he chops up, bundles the firewood with the rope onto his back, delivers it to the outlying hovel of a sick widow. Only after he has lit a fire and warmed the shivering life of the widow does he reappear on the bima to face his congregation and the court of Heaven.

"The Litvak, in Peretz's story, becomes a follower of the *rebbe*. When one of his fellow hasidim is asked by the latest doubting Litvak to reach Nemirov where the *rebbe* goes on the night before Yom Kippur, the hasid answers, 'To Heaven,' and the first Litvak adds, 'If not higher.'

"Kafka's story begins many years later when a third Litvak dares to ask the *rebbe* directly—"

Adrienne jumped out of her chair and ran to the cassette player as if it were Felix himself who was stricken. She pressed the play button once, twice, a third time; it popped back up, the tape had come to its end. "Oh my god," she cried, and grabbing hold of the desk let her legs give way under her; she held on tight as she sank to the floor to counteract the impact, to prevent her aging bones from breaking. She raised her arm in the air and brought down her fist slowly against the cement floor of my office, as if struggling to pull down the handle of a pump, to draw up tears that she couldn't yet feel. She went on repeating this gesture until she cried out in pain, then she stopped, and lay there inert. "Adrienne?" I said softly. She lifted herself off the floor and ran out of the office. I sat there for hours, waiting.

I couldn't reach her for a week. When she returned, she was composed. She told me that Felix hadn't come down for breakfast or lunch on the day after his performance. He had died in his sleep. Belatedly, after the cassette player clicked off, she remembered that she'd interviewed him on the morning of the great day and forgotten to put in a new tape to record the Kafka recital. The tape began rolling with only a few minutes remaining on side B, she'd been so excited as Felix strutted around the stage imitating Jacques Löwy, she hadn't heard the tape recorder shut itself off. Years of work— her most important discovery—lost! How could she not have noticed? She'd gone to the East River and stood at the fence until the light over the city turned from an opaque white to an opaque gray that swallowed the gray of the river. Then she'd gone home and set to work, reconstructing the story of the woodcutter from memory. Some of it was paraphrase; much of it, she said, was close to verbatim. It was clear that she had the sort of prodigious memory upon which the transmission of Tradition depended. She opened her notebook and began reading.

"Kafka's story," she said, "begins where the Peretz story leaves off. It is many years later. A third Litvak arrives and dares to ask the *rebbe* directly, 'Is it true what they say about you?' The Litvak is astonished to find that the *rebbe* has no idea what he is talking about. How can the man be so oblivious? Legends whirl around his name in widening circles that reach as far as Vilna, yet he is innocent of the exalted claims made on his behalf. Such absorption in doing good is beyond the comprehension of the Litvak, and with the righteousness of a proponent of the Haskalah, an enlightener, a man at war with illusion, he tears down the wall of denial behind which the *rebbe* has remained concentrated on his simple task. He takes out his notebook and quotes what people near and far have been saying about the *rebbe*. 'You're a real celebrity,' the Litvak says, as he hands him an article in *Der Yid*, a Yiddish newspaper published in Warsaw; it's a compilation of his sayings that one of his disciples had sent to the editor. The *rebbe* closes his eyes and waits for the Litvak to leave the room.

"While he sits there, frozen by the legend that has devolved into the mystique that opponents of hasidism make the target of their mockery, I want to tell you about the practice that the *rebbe* has evolved between the arrival of the second Litvak and the third. The old widow has died, he has sheltered other widows from the cold, secretly arranged the marriages of orphans, left food on his porch for passing strangers, lain on the graves of the dead and prayed for their release from entanglement with the living. The ax has been replaced by a hidden arsenal of tools and materials: a supply of straw and shingles to repair roofs; a glass cutter; a plumber's snake. Adhering to the ethics of the fathers, the *rebbe* has become skilled as a carpenter, roofer, glazier, plumber; but rather than detain you with an inventory of his accomplishments, each one quite ordinary in itself, let me say that he has become a consummate general contractor. And not only is he a consummate generalist in the realm of construction, he is also the first. But even this does not convey the character of his achievement. Other local artisans of his time have acquired skill in several areas of specialization, but they repair their neighbors' homes out in the open and get paid for the good work they do. Not one of them has understood his task as has the *rebbe* of Nemirov. He has mastered all the crafts needed to repair a house in order to bring about a *yikhud*, a unification among these diverse branches of knowledge and knowledge of the highest order, to remind us that our true aim in building and repairing homes in this world is to provide us with shelter on the way to Paradise. Of him it can be said what Kafka said in praise of another master: 'hammering a table together is to him really hammering together a table, but at the same time it is nothing.' In his own mind, the *rebbe* remains the woodcutter called into the forest by the desire that he could not lay to rest until he lit the fire in the old woman's hearth. He doesn't deny that the woodcutter has developed into a jack-of-all-trades, but to him, that's nothing; at most, in the spirit of the ancient sages who earned their daily bread by manual labor, he thinks of himself as the repairman-*rebbe*.

"But now, after the third Litvak has forced him to confront the sublime image of himself that circulates through the villages and towns of Polish Jewry, the *rebbe*'s whole life is called into question by a voice he recognizes by its needling inflection, a small voice that he has managed to drown out in his prayers, in the fire of good deeds whose tongues of flame sounded in his ears like a flowing stream. Was he no better than the builders of the Tower of Babel, who sought to touch Heaven for the sake of fame? Is that why he had toiled all these years? Had he been keeping this unholy desire a secret from himself as well as everyone else, so that he would be free to build up his name until it became immortal? He remembered a faint sensation of excitement that moved through his body as he went into the woods at midnight; a kind of exaltation seized him as he thought of his congregation standing around and wondering where he was; an image of himself soaring above them flashed by almost too quickly for him to realize what he was thinking. He had to admit that he was not entirely unaware of all the praise he had drawn to himself. When he walked into a room, men of great learning no less than the illiterate ones fell silent and gazed at him with reverence; he would have had to be deaf not to have heard them talking about him as a *tsadek*, a saint. Whatever merit he had gained through his good deeds was stained by his lifelong inability or refusal to live in the truth; his soul was stained by the sin of pride. How could a man with such faults as he now found in himself reach Heaven, and with an ax no less? It was blasphemy to believe that his self-dramatizing display of egolessness had given him greater standing in the eye of God, so that his prayers had opened the gates of Heaven for his hasidim on the Days of Awe. He would have been a truer servant of his community and the Lord if he had performed his anonymous acts of charity in the middle of the work week, and not created a mystery by disappearing at the start of Selichot, setting himself apart from everyone else at the hour of examining one's conscience and submitting oneself to the Judgment by the Almighty. Belatedly, he had come into the knowledge that felt the same as divine punishment. Now there could be no hiding: he would have to be ever-vigilant and struggle against his lust for *koved*. He would have to render a strict account of his every thought to a severe and harassing Master: the Lord of the Law, who spoke to him through conscience.

"Mortified by self-knowledge, the *rebbe* couldn't sleep. All night he studied and prayed; he spent the day in bed, dozing and waking in the darkened room. Even a sliver of light scalded his eyes. He shut them against the day and drifted back to sleep, dreaming of the past when he sailed through clouds. But he could no longer fly in his dreams. He felt himself falling endlessly through space, and awoke in terror. Time slowed to a crawl; he felt stabbing pains up and down his body, and out of these sensations demons emerged with long three-pronged spears tearing at his flesh. Was this a foretaste of what awaited him in the World-to-Come? His wife crept in and left him trays of delicacies. He nibbled, gagged, regurgitated everything but bread and water. How much time passed? He spoke to no one.

"One evening, as he tried to get from his bed to his desk, he tripped and fell. He opened a wound in his forehead.

He lay there without crying out for help. 'Will I die like this?' he wondered. His wife found him, cleaned his wound; the town doctor sewed him up. He nodded yes or no in answer to their questions. It was a relief to be alone again. 'A marked man,' he repeated to himself as he passed himself in the mirror and saw the purple scar on his forehead. He was shocked at how emaciated he had become, his hair had grown long, his beard was wild. He took down the mirror and turned it to the wall. His wife turned away his hasidim, who pleaded with her to let them visit the *rebbe*, if only for a few moments. They became convinced he was dying, they needed to see him for the last time, to say psalms over him and receive his blessing.

"'He is not dying and he will not die,' the *rebetsn* told them. She went about her daily round with a cheerfulness that her neighbors couldn't believe was feigned. 'How is the *rebbe*?' they asked fifty times a day. '*Barukh Hashem*,' she said. And each time she said it, she felt an uprush of faith that dispelled her fear and grief, and she imparted her faith to those around her. With these two words, she upheld the community during the *rebbe*'s absence.

"For the *rebbe*, nothing changed. He made himself get out of bed in the evening and sit before an open book, trying to learn a verse of Torah and pray to the Master of all things who bestows lovingkindness, who supports all who fall, sends healing to the sick, and revives the dead. Without a mirror in which to see himself, he didn't know that the wound in his forehead was fading into a tiny squiggle which was all but hidden by his hair and which his hasidim didn't notice when at last he emerged from his self-imposed prison. At least no one remarked on it. One early morning, as he awoke, he had a reverie of himself back in shul, praying with his congregation. His wife, in response to the wordless communication that goes on between old couples, parted the curtains and let the day into the room; in the pulsing light, a voice that remembered him to life began speaking softly, like his mother, but it was the God from whom he had become estranged, the God who sustains the living with great mercy and causes salvation to flourish. He was jolted by the tenderness he felt in the voice, his trembling body bathed in its stream, became quiet, and he heard it say, 'Murdering yourself in unending acts of self-mortification is a sin far worse than craving a great name.' If the voice had spoken these words harshly, in a tone of rebuke rather than of loving concern, he wouldn't have felt a shock of joy reaching him from the other side of the darkened room where he had shut himself in. It was time to end his penance and return to living his life. As never before, he felt the truth of the Baal Shem Tov's teaching that the heart's affections, rather than a punitive and ascetic spirit, opened the way to Heaven. In using the ax for good works, he had freed the divine sparks trapped in the tool and the firewood it cut, and released them through the fire he built, which brought the warmth of the love of God into the widow's home.

"He knew himself well enough by now to understand that it was his nature to pursue his every aim to excess, so that he had exaggerated the extent of his fault. Wasn't some taint of self-importance inscribed in the human heart by the instinct for self-preservation? This was implicit in the first question which Hillel proposed that he ask himself in weighing his action: if he was not for himself, who would be? In reflecting on his life now, he saw that it hadn't all been vanity. He had gone into the woods feeling concern for the old woman. His service had been genuine.

"Now, as before, he took heart from his desire to serve his community. But what did that mean in this situation?

Should he disillusion his people? Why else had he been given his compassion and intelligence if not to be of use to the people around him? He felt strengthened when they came to him for healing and counsel; they summoned the healer-*rebbe* in him, he made their precarious existence more bearable. Should he rob them of their gratitude and reverence for him, qualities which sweetened their lives? They clung to their image of him because it uplifted them, helped them survive their times of affliction. Yet he demanded of himself that he live in the truth. He was still tempted to view everything he had been and done as impure. Alien thoughts intruded, the old lust for glory surged up, leading him to disavow his life's work. He was being tested by the demon that drove him to extremes. He had to bear his imperfection—truly he had reveled in the thought of his spiritual greatness— without nullifying the caring attention that actually marked his works and days. He had to live with his dark secret, his intimate knowledge of sin and despair. Even now, he wanted to be a *nistar*, a hidden saint, or at least a visible one, a giant of his generation, one of the righteous who bring belief in the coming of the messiah down to earth through acts of compassion, acts in which others may recognize the messianic leanings of their own heart. The task before him now was to hold reality and compassion in a single thought. When he tried bringing such balance into judging himself as he was, here and now, he had to concede that he was a rabbi, a working rabbi, neither more nor less.

"His jaws ached; as usual, he was grinding his teeth. Why couldn't he get past the hunger that gnawed at him? He felt a twinge of nausea, yawned, and got back into bed. There, he floated amidst the phantasmagoria of images; scenes of his life reeled past him, everything he saw made him shudder— until he fell into a deep sleep. He awakens exhausted.

"It is evening; he is ready to take the next step that until now he has driven out of his mind. It is not enough to confess his sins to God; he must put it all into ordinary language and speak it aloud in this world to a person he has deceived, lied to, betrayed. Alone and in silence, he will never be able to move beyond the pride that lures him back into an unreal and isolate existence, locked up in his cell of wounded grandeur.

"With what incredulity he sees everything now. Despite his practice of humility, he has gone on wanting the good people of Nemirov to think of him as a holy man, and more than that, as holier than the sages of Vilna. Lord help him, what unbelievable arrogance! A great pride still remained hidden in him, hidden even from himself. Yet when he enters the dark wood at the edge of town, when he performs the *mitsve* of gathering firewood for the sick widow, he feels himself to be holy through and through. Nonetheless, in his recent illness, he felt the Judgment of Heaven go against him.

"He accepts his fate and calls in his Litvak, the first one, the one he seduced into thinking that he brings the teaching of the Torah to Life.

"Over the years, he has learned to rely on this Litvak who, despite his devotion to the *rebbe*, has retained his *Litvakishe* character, his objective temperament, his logical approach to difficulties; he retrains his yearning from getting in the way of his lucidity. As the *rebbe* lies in his daybed, propped up on his left elbow, he lays out what he has discovered about himself during his illness. But rather than let himself die of the truth, he has come back to the world, only to find himself in an impossible situation. The night of Selichot is approaching. What is he to do now? Go on with the old disappearing act? Disillusion everyone who believes that he flies to Heaven? His face falls into his hand, and when he lifts it up, he looks to the Litvak with pleading eyes.

"The Litvak grasps what's in the *rebbe*'s wordless appeal. He is helpless, his predicament is too much for him. He faces a choice he has evaded all his life, a choice he can barely name: either to betray himself and live a lie, according to the conventions of his place, trafficking in the magical beliefs of the hasidic masses, or, on the other hand, betray his community, deprive them of the miracle that, he realizes now with a heightened feeling for their great vulnerability, sustains them in exile. How can he find his way out of this impasse? The Litvak doesn't ponder the question for more than a moment. Sitting at the *rebbe*'s bedside, under which he hid nearly a quarter of a century ago when he had a choice to make between assimilation and turning his back on the Enlightenment, the Litvak tells the *rebbe* that the people have endured too many false messiahs; that he stands between their vigorous way of life and the memory of catastrophe; that their faith, while strong, is not shockproof; that a generation of young people may be lost if he closes the path to Paradise that leads through the forest at the edge of town.

"'Come,' says the Litvak, 'it is time to leave your sick-bed. I will help you dress.' He goes to the closet where, in years past, the *rebbe* hid the peasant's clothes, and he removes the silken kaftan, the white socks, the black slippers and fur-trimmed hat. Slowly, he helps the *rebbe* put on his holiday attire. He escorts him to the simple wooden table where the *rebbe* sits when he holds court. Standing before him, where petitioners and disciples stand when they ask him to decide a case or offer them counsel, the Litvak issues the following judgment: 'The *rebbe* of Nemirov has only one choice. He must find his way back to Heaven, and with nothing more than the original ax. And this life must be lived with all the powers that he commands until the age of one hundred and twenty years, for it will take all his strength and years to turn the hope he once gave into a reality.'

"With a bowed head, the *rebbe* receives his life-sentence."

*

In those days, I wanted nothing more than to help Adrienne bring her work to a successful conclusion. I volunteered to transcribe the taped portion of Felix's performance and proofread her reconstructed text, a menial task but one whose meaning as support counted for more than the few hours of labor that I was able to subtract from her workload. Two days later, when she came back to pick up the tape and texts, she was still wearing the dress—the baggy black dress—in which I had last seen her. She looked sleep-deprived, disheveled. She kept pulling her glasses off her face and putting them back on. The pleasure I expected to have in handing the finished work over to her seemed suddenly out of place. Without knowing what I was doing or why I was doing it, I too began putting my glasses on and off. Perhaps I thought that if I blurred my sight I would be able to hear better. The whole time that she was talking, I was distracted by a fly buzzing against the window pane, trying to get out. Only afterward, when the room was quiet, was I able to take in what she said. After running from my office, she had gone through a terrible time that ended with her congratulating herself on having reconstructed one of Kafka's lost stories. All that she wanted to do with the euphoria she felt was put it to work. She sat down to edit a transcript of one of her interviews with Dita Hirsch. But somehow the words of the text, like bits of colored glass in a kaleidoscope, shifted, and something emerged that shook her up. She realized, to her horror, that she, like Max Brod, had failed to heed a dying man's wishes, and in fact had sinned against the memory and spirit of the writer whom she most venerated. Belatedly, she saw that anyone who seeks to build their work on Kafka's becomes, like Kafka, conscious of themselves as a Litvak who watches over and torments a rabbi.

APPENDIX
TO THE PROCEEDINGS
OF THE KAFKA CONFERENCE

The Hypnoidal Storyteller:
Kafka Between Two Worlds
Daniel Bergson, M.D.

Over the past forty years, psychology and brain science
have made tremendous advances in our understanding of
the state of mind in which we produce images. We call it
hypnoidal, derived from hypno-, the Greek rootword for
sleep, closely related to hypnosis. It is the gray zone in which
consciousness drifts between waking and sleeping; and it
is this state of absorption in which images came to Kafka
unbidden from whence he knew not where. But one thing he
knew beyond all doubt: he was born for this floating of the
mind in which he crossed over between worlds. He named
his first book *Meditation* after the state of mind in which he
wrote its disparate pieces—the hypnoidal state in which he
watched the images given to him unfold in their own way
and attain an almost mystical depth. On the night that he
wrote "The Judgment" in a single sitting, he had a kind of
conversion experience, his divided self was contained in a
unified narrative, he acquired faith in his practice of hypnoidal
storytelling. This faith never left him, even as he kept losing
and finding his way back to the realm of his sacred journeying
at greater and greater intervals throughout a life spent waiting
for the return of inspiration.

Kafka, like other great early twentieth century
novelists, forged a private religion of writing. In his variant
of the artist's secular sphere of the spirit, inspiration was
christened meditation and pursued simultaneously as a literary
and a spiritual practice. The experience that linked them, in
Kafka's life and work, was the hypnoidal process. From "The

Street Window" in *Meditation* to the last scene in *The Trial*, Kafka travels in the emptiness between attachment and non-attachment to his desire for the outstretched arm of heaven and his desire to be part of the traffic of the world outside his walled-in existence. Here is the complete text of "The Street Window": "Whoever leads a solitary life and yet now and then wants to attach himself somewhere, whoever, according to changes in the time of day, the weather, the state of his business and the like, wishes to see any arm at all to which he might cling—he will not be able to manage for long without a window looking onto the street. And if he is in the mood of not desiring anything and only goes to his window sill a tired man, with eyes turning from his public to heaven and back again, not wanting to look out and having thrown his head up a little, even then the horses below will draw him down to their train of wagons and tumult, and so at last into the human harmony."[1]

The hypnoidal state is produced by dissociation. A flashing up of subliminal consciousness, it comes and goes by day and by night. Most of us ignore its disruption of the apparent unity and continuity of our lives, but Kafka was extremely sensitive to its sudden arrivals and departures; he not only paid close attention to it, he placed great value on the way it belied appearances and drained the world of its solidity, offering access to the desert-labyrinth in which his exodus from bondage took place. He was drawn to track a process that still remains mysterious to most people. Just as Molière's bourgeois gentleman is astounded to learn that he is speaking prose, most of us are surprised to find out that dissociation is a normal process that we undergo every day: it is the capacity of mind that allows us to fall asleep. In order to rest and be refreshed, the mind must be shielded from external stimuli; and so, as my colleague Peter Goldberg has described it, "the mind withdraws from the sensorium."[2] The reasoning sites of the cerebral cortex disconnect from the pathways to the five senses, and surrender to a refuge from labor created by the hallucinatory or image-making power activated by the lower, subcortical brain, the part of the psyche which clinical workers such as myself associate with the deep mind. In healthy persons, such images create safe passage through an internal world founded on the caring arms in which, as a little one, the adult sank into sleep after a good feed in a time before memory. But Kafka, in falling asleep, encountered images that startled him into wakefulness—"a horrible apparition of a blind child," "a donkey that looked like a greyhound [with] narrow human feet... this donkey had never yet gone on all fours but held itself erect like a human being and showed its silvery shining breast and little belly."[3] Exhausted, he fled from the half-sleep in which he was appalled but also overstimulated by what he found there: the truth and creative power of images that showed him his malformed, defective self caught up in situations that defeated him. After three sleepless nights in a row, he wrote: "vivid dreams keep me awake. I sleep alongside myself, so to speak, while I must struggle with dreams. About five the last trace of sleep is exhausted, I just dream, which is more exhausting than wakefulness. In short, I spend the whole night in that state in which a healthy person finds himself for a short time before really falling asleep."[4] And several days later: "Again it was the power of my dreams, shining forth in wakefulness, even before I fall asleep, which did not let me sleep. In the evening and morning my consciousness of the creative abilities in me is more than I can encompass."[5]

In trauma-wracked people, dissociation is taken up as

a defense against a hostile environment that belongs as much to the individual's internal world as to the early environment in which he was condemned to live. This defense takes over a person's days, where it safeguards the mind's lucidity by isolating the capacity to remain rational and vigilant, segregated from the person's sense of self, which is bound up with feelings and sensations that threaten to overwhelm him. In this way, a dissociated ability to think one's way out of destruction is not destroyed. Kafka turned the defense he was stuck with into something else, something compensatory, by seizing its involuntary production of images on behalf of his personally-lived aims, consciously deploying their tremendous power in the way that Perseus used his shield—to mirror, resist and triumph over the power that would have otherwise turned him to stone.

The interpretation of Kafka's work that was prevalent during the middle of the last century saturated the idea of the Kafkaesque with the meaning it continues to name for us. Between the rise of the Third Reich and the fall of the Berlin wall, Kafka's work was widely read as a prophecy of the sociopolitical conditions that render existence absurd; his art was "all the rage" because its nightmarish situations foreshadowed the bureaucratic domination of life under totalitarian rule.[6] Nothing better exemplifies dissociation as a defense against total institutions, in Goffman's phrase, than the use that prisoners of concentration camps made of it. Their chance of surviving one more day, then another, then the day after that, was improved if they unlinked the cognitive function from the self that feels and senses the environment. The mind's split-off lucidity could go on keeping track of the dangers around it and calculating the best moves with which to meet them, like the underground creature in "The Burrow," if it tuned out the stench of burning corpses and the excrement in the open-pit latrines over which the prisoners had to squat on planks from which they sometimes slipped and drowned in their own excrement. There was no escaping the smell of their approaching death anywhere in the camp. The prisoners had to retreat inward, to a realm of thinking whose one aim was survival under working conditions organized to kill them piecemeal before they were finally done away with; then they would be disposed of as so much garbage, just as the charwoman who works for the Samsas removes Gregor's emaciated copse from the premises, out of sight of the family members, who deny any interest in Gregor's fate, refuse to listen to the farcical account that the charwoman is eager to impart to them, and seem to go on with business as usual. But they are in fact renewed and reinvigorated by having the vermin ghettoized, starved and finally made to disappear from their home.

Kafka has rightly been recognized as the first imaginative writer to grasp the role of bureaucracy in modern life. What has been glossed over is his insight that bureaucracy fosters and normalizes dissociation; it values instrumental reason at the expense of all other values and human faculties. His personal experience of hypnoidal states awakened him to the other side of dissociation, the images that represent the cost of cutting the affective-sensory self off from instrumental reason; images that exposed the silvery shining breast and underbelly of the donkey that walked around on two legs like a human being—his double self-images contained traces of his creative potential and gave him the singular lexicon and inspiration which made it possible for him to produce a poetic representation of the bureaucratized daily round. In the fate of Gregor Samsa, Kafka portrays the horror of the modern work world and the horror of dissociation, which, in extreme cases, ends in the thing that most terrified Kafka—madness, loss of one's individual human self, depersonalization. The two kinds of horror are inseparably bound together in the form-and-content unity of the story, which arises out of the loathsome image of the self into which Gregor finds himself transformed. The gigantic insect is an image of depersonalization.

Scholars have interpreted the gigantic insect as a symbol of the passive-aggressive son, or the transgressive artist, or the Jew who refuses assimilation—what Kafka called "the matter-of-fact Jew" of the hasidic heartland. These interpretations name the autobiographical and historical sources of the image, and do away with its horror and enigmatic density. The categorical segmentation of the image into aspects of its origin in real life betrays the reality that the members of the Samsa family and Gregor's Managing Director are forced to confront: Gregor has become an enormous insect, some sort of beetle (the charwoman calls him a dung beetle). What lies entirely beyond the comprehension of the humans in the story is that this is a beetle with a human consciousness. Only the reader is granted privileged access to the stream of reverie that continues to flow through Gregor's memory and imagination. In this way Kafka represents a theme that obsessed him but that has eluded representation in all but the greatest works of art that raise dramatic irony into a form of meditation on the problem of illusion and self-knowledge. In Gregor's inability to recognize and coordinate his physical body and sensations, in the disconnect between his creaturely life and his mentation, Kafka stages a horror show, somewhere between slapstick and tragedy, that compels the reader to face something unheard and unseen by the characters in the story and by most people in everyday life—what Kafka understood as "the split between being and consciousness."[7]

A major task of Kafka criticism has been to interpret this gap. Some scholars have seen it has something intrinsic to human life, the blindness of the metaphysical or the Oedipal seeker after truth; others have viewed it as something imposed by cultural commonsense, the false consciousness that can be changed by a revolution in values and social conditions. The idea of illusion grounded in the evil that enters human life through the Fall, and of repression grounded in ideology or Freudian metapsychology, have prevailed as the explanations of the spiritual, social and psychological condition that Kafka sought to explore in his fiction and philosophical reflections. Yet the Kafkan gap between being and consciousness can also be understood in another way—as the state of dissociation that makes Gregor a stranger to himself and to his real conditions of existence both before and after his metamorphosis.

The story of Gregor's fate begins at the end of a long process of arrested development and breakdown leading to the crisis that kills him. That process has been disavowed in his family and workplace, and has quietly exploited, humiliated and deformed him outside of his own awareness. Before he wakes up to find himself trapped in the body of a man-sized insect, he has identified with the roles of good son and good employee in which the human meaning, coherence and worth of his life have been defined. With the abrupt emergence of his dissociated experience in somatic form, his collusion with those who demand his subservience is no longer possible. Starting with this bizarre *donnée*, Kafka remains faithful to the relations that would "naturally" arise between such a contemptible creature and the persons in whose midst "it" lives. In this way, the story adheres to Kafka's own practice of tracking the image as it changes shape in the alter-world of his reverie.

And what is gained by reading the story as the art of the hypnoidal storyteller can be summed up as follows: Kafka finds his subject broken among dissociative phenomena, and works up the divisive process into the form his story takes, creating its sense of resonant depth, formal perfection, tremendous impact and normalization of shock. The horror of Gregor's life and death is rendered intimate and strange because key aspects of his work world and family life are represented in and through the medium of dissociation. Kafka confines his representation of Gregor's life outside his room to Gregor's split consciousness, to the human consciousness of the beetle. He hardly sleeps, lives in a permanently dissociative state, haunted by the idea of resuming his former position as the breadwinner of the family and by memories of his days and nights as a traveling salesman.[8] The strangeness of that life is made stranger still—more fleeting, fragmented and insubstantial—by its refraction through Gregor's reverie, the hypnoidal realm in which "unapproachable" strangers and colleagues appear for a moment and vanish.[9] His weird condition disrupts verisimilitude—the appearances demanded by the order of everyday life—to reveal the reality of his false relations with himself and his world. Gregor is whirled about in disjointed self-states, oscillating between hope and despair, longing and rage. No passage better exemplifies Kafka's raising dissociation into "lyrical work" and narrative strategy than this one:[10] "Gregor spent his days and nights almost entirely without sleeping. Sometimes he thought about taking the family's affairs in hand again, just as he used to, the next time his door was opened; once more his boss and [the Managing Director] would appear before his mind's eye after all this time, the clerks and the apprentices, the dull-witted hired man, two or three friends from other firms, a chambermaid from a provincial hotel (a sweet, fleeting specter), the shopgirl from a haberdashery whom he had courted earnestly but too slowly—all of these now appeared to him, interspersed with strangers or people already forgotten, but instead of coming to his aid and that of his family, every last one of them was unapproachable, and he was glad when they disappeared. At other times he would be not at all in a frame of mind to look after his family; instead he was filled with rage at how poorly he was attended to, and although he could not imagine anything he would have liked to eat, he plotted how he might gain access to the pantry so as to help himself to what—despite his total absence of hunger—was his due."[11]

In his letters and diaries, Kafka textually pursued the intimacy that he was incapable of sustaining, let alone communicating directly, in his friendships and sexual relationships. Elias Canetti remarks that *The Metamorphosis* is even more intimate than his letters to Felice, and that this quality—the unsurpassed reach of its intimacy—makes it different from any other story he wrote. This intimacy, I suggest, was attained through Kafka's portrayal of his dreamlike inner life and by his self-portrait in the guise of the dutiful employee-son who retreats into his closed hypnoidal room, where he and the reader catch glimpses of the workaday life that made him what he is. A life ruled by the clock. Conversation at the dinner table eaten up by money worries. A harsh regime of worker surveillance that extends to every waking hour of the day and doesn't end at the door of the office. Huge family debt that requires the son to become an indentured servant of his father's creditor, his boss. The chief of the firm sits on his desk, so that his always compliant employee can plainly see their hierarchical relationship and respond with a more thoroughgoing submissiveness. A life hurried and harried by his internalization of the chief's expectations. Collusion with the family that unthinkingly exploits his labor and love on their behalf, to the detriment of the family members. Alignment of the family with the ethos of the commercial enterprise. His mother tells the chief clerk (literally the Managing Director in the German) when he comes to investigate why the employee who claims to be so devoted is in fact two hours late, "The office is the only thing that boy ever thinks of."[12] He suffers from the isolation and deprivation of the business traveler who has no independent life, few friends, no lovers, whose only sexual relationship was with a chambermaid in a rural hotel. The entire field of his sadomasochistic relations with his superiors at his firm and his family is epitomized by the image of a woman in fur which he covers with his body in his effort to protect it from his sister. "He sat there on his picture and would not give it up. He'd sooner leap right in [his sister's] face."[13] She shakes her fist at him, the gesture through which she emerges as the power that will free the family of any residual inhibition against concluding that they must be rid of him. Later, when she strikes the table and declares that "we have to try to get rid of it," Gregor hears this as his death sentence, and he relieves them of the dirty work of carrying it out, using what little life remains to him to let himself die.[14]

Gregor dies as he has lived: in the gap between being and consciousness, withdrawn from the outside world, and partly shielded from his mental and physical pain by dissociation. He had been seriously weakened by the wound he received when his father bombarded him with apples; one of them broke through his carapace, and he has been carrying the rotting apple in his back ever since. Covered with dust, fluff, hair and remnants of food, already grotesque, he has grown more disgusting over time, and has merely exhausted himself as much as his family by his futile efforts of resistance. In the end, he no longer has to be driven back into his room;

he crawls back into it, feeling shame and guilt at making his sister's and parents' lives unbearable. He hears his sister bolt and lock the door. "'And now?' Gregor wondered, looking around in the dark. He soon made the discovery that he was no longer capable of moving at all. He wasn't surprised at this; on the contrary, it struck him as unnatural that he had actually until now been able to support himself on those thin little legs. As for the rest, he felt relatively at ease. Admittedly his entire body was racked with pain, but it had seemed to him as if it was gradually growing weaker and weaker and in the end would fade away altogether. Already he could scarcely feel the rotting apple in his back, and the inflamed area surrounding it, both now enveloped with soft dust. He thought back on his family with tenderness and love. His opinion that he must by all means disappear was possibly even more emphatic than that of his sister. He remained in this state of empty, peaceful reflection until the clock tower struck the third hour in the morning. He watched as everything began to lighten outside his window. Then his head sank all the way to the floor without volition and from his nostrils his last breath faintly streamed."[15]

Notes

The author is indebted to Ritchie Robertson's analysis of the theme of alienated work in *The Metamorphosis*. See *Kafka: Judaism, Politics, and Literature* (Oxford: Clarendon Press, 1985), 74-86.

1. Franz Kafka, "The Street Window," *The Penal Colony: Stories and Short Pieces,* translated by Willa and Edwin Muir (New York: Schocken Books, 1970), 39. Hereafter *Penal Colony*.
2. Peter Goldberg, "Successful Dissociation, Pseudovitality and Inauthentic Use of the Senses," *Psychoanalytic Dialogues* (vo. 5, no. 3, 1995), 496.

3. Franz Kafka, *Diaries*, 10/29/1911, translated by Joseph Kresh (New York: Schocken Books, 1948), 94. Hereafter *Diaries*.

4. *Diaries*, 10/2/1911, 60.

5. *Diaries*, 10/3/1911, 62.

6. Anatole Broyard's memoir of literary life in Greenwich Village in the late 1940s is titled *Kafka Was All the Rage* (New York: Vanguard Books 1997).

7. Ritchie Roberton, *Kafka: Judaism, Politics, and Literature* (Oxford: Clarendon Press, 1985), 82.

8. Franz Kafka, *The Metamorphosis*, translated by Susan Berofsky (New York: W.W. Norton & Company, 2014), 90-91. Hereafter *Metamorphosis*.

9. Ibid.

10. Reiner Stach, *Kafka: The Decisive Years*, translated by Shelley Frisch (Princeton: Princeton University Press, 2013), 291. See *Diaries*, 10/3/1911, 82.

11. *Metamorphosis*, 90-91.

12. *Metamorphosis*, 34.

13. *Metamorphosis*, 78.

14. *Metamorphosis*, 105.

15. *Metamorphosis*, 109-110.

GLOSSARY

This book uses standard Yiddish according to the Institute for Jewish Research (YIVO) transliteration system. Words from languages other than Yiddish are indicated as (H) Hebrew and (G) German.

A gilgul fun a nign Literally, a metempsychosis of a melody. The name of a story by I.L. Peretz about the transmigration of a melody from religious life through secular streets and performances back to its use in hasidic ritual.

Baal teshuvah (H) Literally, a master of repentance. Among hasidim, a Jew who has become a newly observant member of their sect.

Barukh Hashem Literally, Blessed be the Name. In reading sacred texts and in conversation, hasidic and ultra-Orthodox Jews do not utter the name of God, but refer to YHWH as *Hashem*, the Name.

Besmedresh Prayer and study house; small orthodox synagogue.

Bokher A religious student; a young man.

Bontshe Shveyg Literally, Bontshe the Silent. The name of the self-effacing good person and the title of the story by I.L. Peretz that celebrates his saintliness and critiques his submissiveness.

Genizah (H) A hiding place or store room, usually connected with a synagogue, for the deposition of worn-out scrolls and sacred books.

Judengassen (G) Literally, Jews' streets. The Jewish quarter.

Judenrat (G) Jewish Council. In each of the ghettos, the Nazis set up a *Judenrat* to carry out their directives.

Khazonish In the manner of a *khazon*, a cantor.

Kheder Traditional Jewish elementary school.

Koved (H) Honor.

Kushia (H) A difficulty. In Talmudic discussion, an argument that threatens to resolve a controversy is considered a difficulty.

Lamed Vavnik One of the Thirty-Six Righteous Men. According to the Talmud and Jewish legend, the continued existence of humanity depends upon the merit of the thirty-six men of humble vocation whose spiritual gifts are unrecognized in this world.

Litvakishe Adjectival form of *Litvak*, Lithuanian.

Luftmentsh Literally, an air-person. A dreamer, someone with his head in the clouds; a person without any definite occupation.

Melamed A teacher of children.

Mitsve A commandment of the Jewish Law. The term is also used to refer, more broadly, to a good deed.

Narishkeit Foolishness.

Nistar A hidden saint.

Ostjuden (G) Eastern European Jews.

Peyes Literally, "corners" of the beard. Earlocks left uncut by pious Jews.

Rebbe of Mezritsh The Baal Shem Tov, founder of Hasidism.

Selichot (H) Penitential prayers

Shabes The Sabbath.

Shames Attendant in a synagogue, rabbi's personal assistant.

Sheytl A wig worn by an observant Jewish woman.

Shmates Rags.

Shvitzbod Turkish bath, steambath.

Teruz (H) A solution. In Talmudic discussion, an argument that restores the controversy is considered a solution.

Tsadek A righteous man; a hasidic rabbi.

Yiddische kinderlach (Kafka's transliteration of the Yiddish phrase) little Jewish kids.

Yikhud (H) A unification.

BIBLIOGRAPHY

Works by Kafka

Diaries, 1910-1923. Edited by Max Brod. *Diaries 1910-13.*
Translated by Joseph Kresh. *Diaries 1914-23.* Translated
by Martin Greenberg. New York: Schocken Books, 1948.
Hereafter *Diaries*.

Letter to His Father. Translated by Ernst Kaiser and Eithne
Wilkins. New York: Schocken Books, 1953. Hereafter *Father*.

Letters to Felice. Translated by James Stern and Elizabeth
Duckworth. New York: Schocken Books, 1973. Hereafter
Felice.

Letters to Friends, Family, and Editors. Translated by Richard
and Clara Winston. New York: Schocken Books, 1977.
Hereafter *Friends*.

Letters to Milena. Edited by Willi Haas. Translated by Tania
and James Stern. New York: Schocken Books, 1953. Hereafter
Milena.

The Blue Octavo Notebooks. Translated by Ernst Kaiser and
Eithne Wilkins. Cambridge: Exact Change, 1991. Hereafter
Notebooks.

The Castle. Translated by Mark Harman. New York:
Schocken Books, 1998. Hereafter *Castle*.

The Trial. Translated by Willa and Edwin Muir. New York:
Vintage Books, 1969. Hereafter *Trial*.

The Great Wall of China: Stories and Reflections. Translated by Willa and Edwin Muir. New York: Schocken Books, 1970. Hereafter *Great Wall*.

The Metamorphosis. Translated by Susan Bernofsky. New York: W.W. Norton & Company, 2014. Hereafter *Metamorphosis*.

Paradoxes and Parables. Translated by Willa and Edwin Muir, and Others. New York: Schocken Books, 1976. Hereafter *Parables*.

The Penal Colony: Stories and Short Pieces. Translated by Willa and Edwin Muir. New York: Schocken Books, 1961. Hereafter *Penal Colony*.

Selected Short Stories of Franz Kafka. Translated by Willa and Edwin Muir. New York: The Modern Library, 1952. Hereafter *Selected Stories*.

BIOGRAPHY AND CRITICISM

Anderson, Mark. "Introduction," "Unsigned Letters to Milena Jesenská." In *Reading Kafka: Prague, Politics, and the Fin de Siècle*. Edited by Mark Anderson. New York: Schocken Books, 1989. Hereafter *Reading Kafka*.

Benjamin, Walter. "Franz Kafka: On the Tenth Anniversary of His Death," "Reflections on Kafka." In *Illuminations*. Edited and with an Introduction by Hannah Arendt. Translated by Harry Zohn, New York: Schocken Books, 1969. Hereafter *Illuminations*.

-----------, "Review of Brod's *Franz Kafka*," "Letter to Gershom Scholem on Franz Kafka." In *Walter Benjamin: Selected Writings, Vol. 3, 1935-1938*. Edited by Howard Eiland and Michael W. Jennings. Translated by Edmund Jephcott, Howard Eiland, and Others. Cambridge: The Belknap Press, 2002. Hereafter *WB: Selected Writings*.

Brod, Max. *Franz Kafka: A Biography*. Translated by G. Humphreys Roberts and Richard Winston. New York: Schocken Books, 1963. Hereafter *Kafka: A Biography*.

Canetti, Elias. *Kafka's Other Trial: The Letters to Felice*. Translated by Christopher Middleton. New York: Schocken Press, 1974. Hereafter *Other Trial*.

Deleuze, Gilles and Felix Guattari. *Kafka: Toward a Minor Literature*. Translated by Dana Polan. Minneapolis: University of Minnesota Press, 1986. Hereafter *Minor Literature*.

Friedlander, Saul. *Franz Kafka: The Poet of Shame and Guilt*. New Haven: Yale University Press, 2013. Hereafter *FK: Poet*.

Goodman, Paul. *Kafka's Prayer*. New York: Stonehill Publishing Company, 1947.

Pawel, Ernst. *The Nightmare of Reason: A Life of Franz Kafka*. New York: The Noonday Press, 1984. Hereafter *Nightmare*.

Stach, Reiner. *Kafka: The Decisive Years*. Translated by Shelley Frisch. Princeton: Princeton University Press, 2013. Hereafter *Decisive Years*.

----------. *Kafka: The Years of Insight*. Translated by Shelley Frisch. Princeton: Princeton University Press, 2013. Hereafter *Years of Insight*.

Robert, Marthe. *As Lonely as Franz Kafka*. Translated by Ralph Manheim. New York: Schocken Books, 1986. Hereafter *Lonely as FK*.

Robertson, Ritchie. *Kafka: Judaism, Politics, and Literature*. Oxford: Clarendon Press, 1985. Hereafter *Kafka: JPL*.

SOURCE NOTES

I. HIS ROOM

"A Dry Eye in the House"

"What we need... sea within us": A near-verbatim appropriation of a passage from Kafka's "Letter to Oskar Pollak," 1/27/1904. Translated and quoted by Pawel in *Nightmare*, 158. For entire letter, see *Friends*, 15-16.

"A Stray"

a woman... cap and stole: Based on the picture from an illustrated magazine that Gregor Samsa hangs above his work table. See *Metamorphosis*, 22.

pricks up his ears... to the wall: a near-verbatim appropriation of a passage from Kafka's *Notebooks*, 1.

"The Black Letters"

a break... chain of generations: A near-verbatim appropriation of Kafka's self-indictment in "He," *Great Wall*, 153. Hereafter "He."

... in common with myself?: A reflection appropriated from Kafka's *Diaries*, 1/8/1914, 252.

"Repetition of the Same"

simply running around... confused than before: A near-verbatim appropriation taken from *Milena*, 35.

gnawing at him... hounding him: A near-verbatim appropriation taken from Kafka's *Diaries*, 1/18/1922, 400.

What have you done... gift of sex?: A statement taken from Kafka's *Diaries*, 1/18/1922, 399.

"THE CARD PLAYERS"

Savage beings... formless clamor: A near-verbatim adaptation of a passage from Kafka's *Diaries*, 1/7/1922, 171-172.

unconsciously played the part... in a hunt: A near-verbatim appropriation of a passage from *Father*, 45.

lost the capacity... in his presence: A near-verbatim appropriation of a statement from *Father*, 33.

"THE STORYTELLER"

Put it on my bedside table: An utterance appropriated from Kafka's *Father*, 87.

When Father ran... by his leave: A near-verbatim appropriation of two passages from *Father*, 35, 37.

"IN LIEU OF SUICIDE"

Agonies in bed: A phrase appropriated from Kafka's *Diaries*, 8/15/1913, 228.

throw my suit... let myself sink: Adapted from "The Judgment," *Selected Stories*, 18. Hereafter "Judgment."

Sentenced to death by drowning: A near-verbatim appropriation taken from "Judgment," 18.

make an enemy... to no one: Two phrases appropriated from Kafka's *Diaries*, 8/15/1913, 229.

I'm an atheist... wants me to write: This utterance is adapted from Marthe Robert's discussion of the letter that Kafka wrote to Oskar Pollak on 11/9/1903. See *Lonely as FK*, 37-38. For the letter, see *Friends*, 10.

"God doesn't want me to write:" is a quotation from the letter.

"TOWARD DAWN"

a butcher knife... of my side: A near-verbatim appropriation of a statement from Kafka's "Letter to Max Brod," 4/3/1913. *Friends*, 95.

For all things... a sort of adumbration: A near-verbatim appropriation taken from "Reflections on Sin, Pain, Hope, and the True Way," *Great Wall*, 173. Hereafter "Reflections."

"His Daily Practice"

a tiny harbor... steamers usually call: A near-verbatim appropriation taken from Kafka's *Diaries*, 4/6/1917, 373.

he travels... to stupid imaginations: A near-verbatim appropriation taken from "The Hunter Gracchus," *Selected Stories*, 185-186.

carpentry, Zionism... an apartment of his own: A near-verbatim appropriation taken from Kafka's *Diaries*, 1/23/1922, 409.

If one were only an Indian... be gone: A near-verbatim quotation of "The Wish to Be a Red Indian," *Penal Colony*, 39. Hereafter "Red Indian."

II. BOTCHED REVELATIONS

"In His Father's Warehouse"

This section contains near-verbatim appropriations and freer adaptations of passages taken from Brod's *Kafka: A Biography*. See pp. 5, 6, 8, 9, 22, 23, 163.

wished to be numbered among ordinary men: Walter Benjamin, "Franz Kafka: On the Tenth Anniversary of His Death," *Illuminations*, 124.

a tight-fitting black suit... eminently practical: A near-verbatim appropriation taken from Kafka's *Trial*, 4.

He was so… in every utterance: A near-verbatim appropriation of Canetti, *Other Trial*, 30.

my bonhomie… path to holiness: A near-verbatim appropriation of Benjamin, "Review of Brod's *Franz Kafka*," *WB: Selected Writings*, 317.

the true way… walked along: A near-verbatim appropriation taken from Kafka's "Reflections," 162.

"The Broken Tablets"

This section contains near-verbatim appropriations and freer adaptations of passages taken from Brod's *Kafka: A Biography*. See pp. 12, 104, 105, 124-125, 127, 131-132.

Just when everything… a piece of its flesh: A near-verbatim appropriation taken from Kafka's *Diaries*, 10/3/1911, 62.

III. ASTRAY

"This Deadness"

Evil is whatever distracts: A reflection appropriated from Kafka's *Notebooks*, 24.

that other world… freedom of movement: Adapted from Kafka's *Diaries*, 1/28/1922, 407 and 1/19/1922, 409.

Ach, you metaphors… despair of writing: A near-verbatim appropriation taken from Kafka's *Diaries*, 12/6/1921, 398.

as if a board… my description: A near-verbatim appropriation taken from Kafka's *Diaries*, 12/27/1911, 155.

"His Lateness"

cheeks trembling, then wet: An adaptation of a phrase taken from Kafka's *Diaries*, 10/5/1911, 65.

My mother remembers... named after him: A near-verbatim appropriation of a passage from Kafka's *Diaries*, 12/25/1911, 152-153.

"The Double"

my fishlike emotion: A phrase appropriated from Kafka's *Diaries*, 8/20/1911, 51.

his cousin Khaskel... the temple of Jewish art: An appropriation of Yitzkhok Leyvi's first-person life-story quoted by Kafka in his *Notebooks*, 80-83.

in European clothes... a mourner at a wedding: A phrase in a letter from Yitzkhok Leyvi to his parents quoted by Kafka, *Diaries*, 11/22/1911, 125.

"In the Midst of Yiddish"

And Yiddish is everything... the Jewish actor: A near-verbatim appropriation of Kafka's "Introductory Talk on the Yiddish Language," edited by Mark Anderson, translated by Ernst Kaiser and Eithne Wilkins, in *Reading Kafka*, 266.

"To the Bath House"

In great perplexity: A phrase appropriated from Kafka's story, "A Country Doctor," *Penal Colony*, 136.

"In Search of a Master"

I wait... at each nostril: A near-verbatim appropriation of a passage from Kafka's *Diaries*, 3/28/1911, 48-49.

"In Bed"

a toothless father... delivering judgment: A near-verbatim appropriation of a passage from "The Judgment," *Penal Colony*, 55, 59.

the bucket I ride: An image taken from Kafka's story, "The Bucket Rider," *Penal Colony*, 184.

"His Nausea"

Langer's grown *peyis*… Blatant superstition: An appropriation of a passage from Stach, *Years of Insight*, 107.

I feel helpless… being inconceivable: A near-verbatim appropriation of a passage from Kafka's *Diaries*, 11/27/1913, 242-243.

he need not strive, the operation of nature: An adaptation of two passages from "Reflections," 167, 173.

as if I were confined… walls around me: An appropriation of a passage taken from Kafka's *Trial*, 89.

"A Private Ritual"

I love you… become another person: A near-verbatim appropriation of a statement in a letter to Felice quoted by Kafka in his *Diaries*, 3/19/1914, 263.

"The Heightened Din"

The forms my decline… my parents' bedroom: A near-verbatim appropriation of a passage from Kafka's *Diaries*, 12/2/1917, 387.

Leaden meaningless clouds drift by: A near-verbatim appropriation of a statement from Kafka's *Diaries*, 11/2/1917, 387

Sheer impotence: A phrase taken from Kafka's *Diaries*, 11/6/1917, 389.

Something like a breakdown… the two worlds: A near-verbatim appropriation of a passage from Kafka's *Diaries*, 1/6/1922, 398-399.

"His Futility"

The work awaiting me… in the kitchen: A near-verbatim appropriation of a passage from Kafka's *Diaries*, 11/17/1917, 389 and 2/14/1922, 414.

He hates writing's lack… a joke: A near-verbatim appropriation of a passage from Kafka's *Diaries*, 12/6/1921, 398.

"A Little Phrase"

I can't stand… clients in bed: A near-verbatim appropriation of a passage from Kafka's *Trial*, 23.

I won't say… an obscene world: A near-verbatim appropriation of a passage from *Milena*, 164.

"Voice in the Head He Can't Escape"

do whatever you like… a free hand: A near-verbatim appropriation of a passage from *Father*, 31.

What did she do… sort of fishing: Freely adapted from a passage in *Father*, 107.

Frank I'm sorry… by the hand: Freely adapted from a passage in *Father*, 107.

"Make Him Go Away"

By the light… written down nothing: A near-verbatim appropriation of a passage from Kafka's *Diaries*, 12/20/1921, 398.

"Shocks"

Rejected by sleep… cuts me to pieces unhindered: A near-verbatim appropriation of a passage from Kafka's *Diaries*, 10/2/1922, 60-61.

the pure… the immutable: An appropriation of a series of phrases taken from Kafka's *Diaries*, 9/25/1917, 387.

"Sounds in the Background"
If I'm not mistaken… things about them: A near-verbatim appropriation of a passage from Kafka's *Diaries*, 5/27/1914, 271.

"From the Book of Unfinished Stories"
It became known… to its climax: A near-verbatim appropriation of a passage from Kafka's *Diaries*, 4/19/1916, 360.

V. DISAPPEARING ACTS

"In Kafka's Labyrinth"
What we need… what I believe: An appropriation of a passage from Kafka's "Letter to Oskar Pollak," 1/27/1904. Translated and quoted by Pawel in *Nightmare*, 158.
doesn't shake us… blow to the skull: Ibid.
forced to serve: An appropriation of a phrase from Deleuze and Guattari's *Minor Literature*, 19.

"Independent Scrutiny"
blades that whirl… fingers cut off: A near-verbatim appropriation of "a routine industrial report" that Kafka wrote in 1909. Quoted without citation of its source by Goodman in *Kafka's Prayer*, 126-127.
he hears convulsive sighs… his birch rod: A near-verbatim appropriation of a scene in Kafka's *Trial*, 103-111.
Anyone who can't… fight with despair: A near-verbatim appropriation of a passage from Kafka's *Diaries*, 10/19/1921, 394.

"Reflections in a Jewish Shop window"
Spent all afternoon… filthy rabble: A near-verbatim appropriation taken from *Milena*, 213.

The riot squad... the mob: Ibid.

the shame... out of the bathroom: Ibid.

no one... engages in politics: A near-verbatim appropriation of a statement by Brod in a letter to Kafka. Quoted by Pawel in *Nightmare*, 317.

A long thin creature... a friendly smile: A near-verbatim appropriation from *Milena*, 70.

my 38 Jewish years: An appropriation of a phrase taken from *Milena*, 68.

"THE DESCENT"

the impenetrable outline... it was horrible: A near-verbatim appropriation of a statement taken from Kafka's *Diaries*, 10/30/1921, 396.

when he was away... restoring that fullness: A near-verbatim appropriation of a passage from Kafka's *Diaries*, 11/15/1911, 118.

"HOUSEHOLD GOD"

For every man... the god of suffocation: A near-verbatim appropriation of a passage from Kafka's *Diaries*, 2/1/1922, 410.

never to learn anything useful: A near-verbatim appropriation of a statement taken from Kafka's *Diaries*, 10/17/1921, 393.

allowed myself to become a physical wreck: An insight appropriated from Kafka's *Diaries*, 10/17/1921, 393.

I was too weak... a great distraction: A near-verbatim appropriation of a passage from Kafka's *Diaries*, 10/17/1921, 393.

"THE OTHER HAND"

a man without... a human being: A near-verbatim appropriation of a sentence from the Talmud that Kafka quotes in his *Diaries*, 11/24/1911, 126.

walking around… in a summer suit: A phrase from one of Kafka's letters to Felice. Source can no longer be located.

fasting as the supreme… of his investigations: A near-verbatim appropriation of a statement from *Lonely as FK*, 97.

"Serving the Evil One"

Writing is a sweet… only this one: A near-verbatim appropriation of a passage from Kafka's "Letter to Max Brod," 7/5/1922, *Friends*, 333-334.

"An Incurable Condition"

to be despairing… was on earth: A near-verbatim appropriation of a statement in Kafka's *Diaries*, 10/16/1921, 392.

"The Pigeon"

Everything I saw… a bright tangle: A near-verbatim appropriation of two passages from Kafka's *Diaries*, 11/19/1913, 237, and 11/21/1913, 239.

VI. THE KAFKAN SENTENCE

"The Wood-Burning Stove"

steadfast love: *Diaries*, 10/23/1911, 86.

Some of the songs… my cheeks tremble: A near-verbatim appropriation of a passage from Kafka's *Diaries*, 10/5/1922, 65.

Stolen liturgical melodies… people sing them: Two phrases appropriated from Kafka's *Diaries*, 10/23/1911, 86.

my concentrated energy: A phrase appropriated from Kafka's *Diaries*. Source can no longer be located.

attention is the natural prayer of the heart: A statement of Kafka quoted from memory. Source unknown.

Kafka was far... to its transmissibility: Walter Benjamin appropriated this idea from a passage translated and quoted by Hannah Arendt in her "Introduction" to *Illuminations*, 41.

he read Grimms' fairy tales... out of reach: Based on *Years of Insight*, 517, 528.

Dora recited Havdalah... more for Aggada: Based on *Years of Insight*, 529.

he had tried to write a story... [about] Mendl Beilis: Cited from memory. Source can no longer be located.

"Kafka's Commas"

In general... at the listener: Kafka, a diary passage of 1911, quoted by Mark Harman, "Translator's Preface," in *Castle*, xxi.

If one were only an Indian... be gone: A near-verbatim quotation of "The Wish to Be a Red Indian," *Penal Colony*, 39.

the almost inaudible... wakened [him]: Kafka, "The Burrow," *Selected Stories*, Source cited from memory.

It goes on... a kind of piping: A near-verbatim appropriation of a statement from "Burrow," 256.

must have... loose easy soil: A near-verbatim appropriation of a statement from "Burrow," 258.

And it is not... believe in them: Ibid.

They are creatures... air to breathe: Ibid.

All that can be... natural firm rock: A near-verbatim appropriation of a statement from "Burrow," 256.

When I stand... my castle: A near-verbatim appropriation of a statement from "Burrow," 277.

a state of being… craves suffocation: A near-verbatim appropriation of a statement from "Reflections on Sin, Suffering, Hope, and the True Way," in *Notebooks*, 89.

the beautifully vaulted chamber: A phrase appropriated from "Burrow," 260.

But for such tasks… my Castle Keep: A near-verbatim appropriation of a statement from "Burrow," 260-261.

I am not… my thoughts: A quotation from "Burrow," 268.
blood and soil: A phrase quoted from "Burrow," 277.

then I know… blissful sleep: a phrase quoted from "Burrow," 277.

stoppages of the currents of air: A phrase appropriated from "Burrow," 282.

the technical problem… attracts [him]: A near-verbatim appropriation of a statement from "Burrow," 283.

on fire to discover… can't feel safe: Ibid.

I can find… the explanation be?: A near-verbatim appropriation of a statement from "Burrow," 283-284.

Here in the brief… these performances: Kafka, "Josephine the Singer, or the Mouse Folk," *Penal Colony*, 269.

And yet it wasn't true… raided the apartment: Based on *Years of Thought*, 542-543.

Kafka had stolen… his closest friend: Based on Mark Anderson's "Introduction," *Reading Kafka*, 7, 13.

"Story of the Woodcutter"

like a dandy… and a derby: A near-verbatim appropriation of a passage in I. B. Singer's story, "A Friend of Kafka," in *A Friend of Kafka*. Translated by the author and Elizabeth Shub (New York: Fawcett Crest, 1980), 7.

A NOTE ABOUT THE AUTHOR

MARC KAMINSKY is a poet and retired psychotherapist. He is the author of eight previous books of poetry, including *The Stones of Lifta* (Dos Madres Press), *The Road from Hiroshima* (Simon & Schuster), and *Daily Bread* (University of Illinois Press). His poems, essays and fiction have appeared in many magazines and anthologies, including *The Manhattan Review, The American Scholar, Natural Bridge, The Oxford Book of Aging,* and *Voices within the Ark: The Modern Jewish Poets.* He has published six books on aging, reminiscence and late-life development, and the culture of Yiddishkeit.

OTHER BOOKS BY MARC KAMINSKY
PUBLISHED BY DOS MADRES PRESS

A CLEFT IN THE ROCK (2018)
THE STONES OF LIFTA (2019)

FOR THE FULL DOS MADRES PRESS CATALOG:
www.dosmadres.com

www.ingramcontent.com/pod-product-compliance
Lightning Source LLC
Chambersburg PA
CBHW030911120626
46554CB00001B/102